"IT'S NOT YOUR SOCIAL LIFE... IT ONLY FEELS THAT WAY.

Breaking up is painful... but it won't scar you permanently. *Cosmopolitan* Magazine's GETTING OVER HIM will not only help you survive... it will help you thrive in your new role as *The Single Girl*.

- **Look Around:** There are men everywhere. From the Laundromat to the coffee shop, the dating prospects are right in front of you.
- **Helping Hands & Sympathetic Ears:** The right places to turn for support... and a reality check.
- **Getting Even:** Self-improvement is the best revenge (not mind games).
- **Give Yourself a Break:** Yes, you may have made a bad choice. But remember, everyone has been there.
- **Getting Real:** Are you really dealing with lost love or just sex-deprivation?

GETTING OVER HIM
Cosmopolitan Magazine's Complete Break-Up Survival Handbook

Other **Cosmopolitan Books**

THE NICE GIRL'S GUIDE TO SENSATIONAL SEX
THE BEDSIDE ASTROLOGER COMPANION
IRMA KURTZ'S ULTIMATE PROBLEM SOLVER
WHAT MEN WANT FROM THE WOMEN THEY LOVE
ALL THE GOOD MEN ARE *NOT* TAKEN
IS HE THE RIGHT MAN FOR YOU?
STAR SPELLS
WHY DON'T YOU . . .
THE DATING GAME
WHERE THE BOYS ARE

Cosmopolitan Books are available at special quantity discounts for bulk purchases for sales promotions, premiums, fund raising or educational use. Special books, or book excerpts, can also be created to fit specific needs.

For details write or telephone the office of the Director of Special Markets, Avon Books, Dept. FP, 1350 Avenue of the Americas, New York, New York 10019, 1-800-238-0658.

Getting Over *Him*

Cosmo's Complete Break-Up Survival Handbook

ELIZABETH HURCHALLA

COSMOPOLITAN

The purpose of this book is to educate and entertain. It is sold with the understanding that the publisher and author are not rendering medical, psychological, or other professional services. The publisher and author shall not be liable or responsible to any person or entity with respect to any loss or damage caused or alleged to be caused directly or indirectly by the information that appears in this book. The names of some of the people whose stories appear in this book have been changed to conceal their identities.

COSMOPOLITAN BOOKS
AVON BOOKS
A division of
The Hearst Corporation
1350 Avenue of the Americas
New York, New York 10019

Copyright © 1997 by Cosmopolitan
Published by arrangement with Cosmopolitan
Visit our website at **http://www.AvonBooks.com**
Library of Congress Catalog Card Number: 97-93753
ISBN: 0-380-79398-9

All rights reserved, which includes the right to reproduce this book or portions thereof in any form whatsoever except as provided by the U.S. Copyright Law. For information address Avon Books.

First Cosmopolitan Books Printing: December 1997

COSMOPOLITAN TRADEMARK REG. U.S. PAT. OFF. AND IN OTHER COUNTRIES, MARCA REGISTRADA, HECHO EN U.S.A.

Printed in the U.S.A.

WCD 10 9 8 7 6 5 4 3 2 1

If you purchased this book without a cover, you should be aware that this book is stolen property. It was reported as "unsold and destroyed" to the publisher, and neither the author nor the publisher has received any payment for this "stripped book."

To my parents,
for always being there for me

Acknowledgments

First, I'd like to thank Julie Taylor, who generously offered her suggestions, criticisms, and encouragement throughout the writing of this book. She also spoke to me in detail about her personal breakup experiences, which are recounted at length (albeit in fictionalized form) in her own book, *Franco American Dreams* (Simon & Schuster, 1997). She is a talented editor and a great friend, and I couldn't have done it without her. I'd also like to express my appreciation to Ivy Garcia for her amazing friendship and considerable assistance in organizing this project from the beginning, as well as her astute editing along the way. In addition, George, Jean, Dave, and Jeff Hurchalla have my sincere gratitude for their gracious help and enduring support.

Thanks are also owed to the therapists who so kindly volunteered their time and insights: Dr. Karen Peterson, Sharyn Hillyer, Dr. Kathleen Mojas, Dr. Deborah Cooper, Joan Childs, Dr. David Lutwin, Suzanne Lopez, Dr. Peter Sheras, and Dr. Judy Kuriansky. And likewise to the many people who shared their own breakup stories (those of you who appear with fake names, you know who you are): Diana, Robin, Laura,

Zanni, Darcy, Beth, Karrie, Samantha, Ivy, Virginia, Mick, Bart, Julie, Jeffrey, Leigh, Dawn, Janice, Melissa, Jacqueline, Jenni, Rick, Lana, Missy, Noelle, Jennifer, Steve, Stacey, Lacy, Ashley, Brenda, Traci, Ann, Mavis, Amelia, Abby, Debbie, Rhonda, Catherine, Lizzie, Gail, Jayna, Nancy, Kim, Torry, Lance, Marcie, Kristen, Lori, Caitlin, and Kathy.

I am grateful to my wonderful editor, Nancy Kalish, who is both a true mentor and an all-around pleasure to know. In addition, I'd like to thank David Delp and Torry Davidson for their thoughtful contributions and continuing faith in me. An overdue thank-you goes to Mark Lewman, who believed in me enough to give me my first writing job. Thanks, too, to Elizabeth Nix, Joe L. Batutis, Sue Rabii, Bill Newell, Tia Maggini, and the interns who assisted with this book, Alonna Friedman and Heather Camlot. And finally, I find myself in the ironic position of thanking James, who broke my heart, but in so doing gave me the wisdom of experience that helped make this book what it is.

Contents

Introduction   1

Chapter One
He's Out of Your Life—
And You're Out of Your Mind   6

Chapter Two
Getting Disconnected   25

Chapter Three
What If You Want Him Back?   56

Chapter Four
Okay, You're Still Obsessing   103

Chapter Five
What Went Wrong   136

Chapter Six
Reinventing Yourself   178

Chapter Seven
Starting Over   206

Introduction

Welcome to the end of the fairy tale. I know, I know, the two of you were living so happily ever after, too—that is, until he ran off with his personal trainer. Or decided he was too young to get tied down. Or landed that couldn't-pass-it-up job in Tanzania. Or whatever. In any case, he's ditched you.

Or maybe you've ditched him—but only because he forced you into it by cheating on you repeatedly. Or calling you bimonthly when he used to call hourly. Or telling you after eight years of dating that he had no intention of ever walking down the aisle with you. Regardless of the details of your own personal breakup saga, one thing's clear: You're hurting as sure as if your entire body were covered with third-degree burns.

Believe me, I know how you feel. My heart has been broken, too. But I've managed to stitch it back together and apply a little glue here and there, so you can hardly even tell anymore. Of course, I remember. Like all walking wounded, I have my war story.

In July of 1995, I took a trip to Sydney for ten days. Because I went with my brother, who worked for United Airlines, the flight was less than $400 round-trip—an enticing offer any way you look at it, but particularly appealing to me because I hadn't seen James, my Aussie boyfriend of more than five years, for almost a year and a half. James was saving up to move to the States, but in the meantime we spoke often on the phone and wrote hundreds of letters back and forth about how much we missed each other. Since the whole Australia trip was last-minute anyway, I decided not to tell him I was coming; instead, I thought, I'd surprise him at his front door. To make sure he got time off work, I had his sister tell him she'd won a trip to Fiji for two and wanted him to go along. Everything was set. As I packed my bags, I couldn't have been more excited.

When I got there, James kept laughing and saying he couldn't believe it. He gave me a big kiss and hug and we lay on his bed and talked. I asked him if he'd been dating anyone. (We had an agreement that we could see other people when we were apart, but I'd gone out on only one date during that entire year and a half.) To my shock, he said yes; in fact, she had been starting to get serious, but then he had told her about me and broken it off. Even though he wasn't still seeing her, I felt hurt, upset; I wanted to know who she was. Before long, James started saying maybe it hadn't been such a good idea to surprise him. After all, we hadn't seen each other in over a year, and already we were having a fight. Maybe it would have been better if we had both been able to prepare ourselves for this meeting. I couldn't believe I had come all that way for him to complain about the fact that he wasn't expecting me. Trying to work out plans for the rest of my stay only added to the tension. We found ourselves snapping at each other; at dinner that night, we barely spoke.

Things went downhill from there. I spent much of the week and a half crying and saying, "We're going to break up, aren't we?" I knew I was being clingy, but I was so desperate for reassurance that I couldn't help myself. Before my trip, James had been saying he wanted to move to New York by December, but suddenly that was turning into the following summer, or maybe later—it was hard to say. When I left, he bought me a box of chocolate-covered macadamia nuts at the airport, and we both cried and said "I love you" and hugged for a long, long time. But during our long-distance phone conversations over the next few weeks, it became clear that our relationship was coming to an end. He didn't say so in those exact words—there was a lot of "Well, let's see how things go, see how we feel, I need some time"— but when I finally said "So I guess I was right. We *are* breaking up, huh?" he acknowledged that, yeah, maybe we were. I was devastated. I pleaded with him over the phone. I lost weight. I burst into tears at work. I started to imagine myself climbing out of my sixth-story window.

This man had written me poetry, made me birthday cakes from scratch, left his family and friends for years at a time to be with me. I had lived with him in Los Angeles and London, traveled with him all over the United States and Europe, fantasized about us building a life together in New York. I thought I would marry him. I thought I'd have a family with him. I thought I'd be with him forever. My identity was so wrapped up in being half of this couple that suddenly I didn't know who I was. My whole future had been erased.

But now, a year and a half later, through the help of friends, family, and a lot of self-reflection, I've accepted the breakup and gotten on with my life. Unfortunately, I held on to the pain longer than I should have—more on that later—but thanks to the benefit of my experience, plus plenty of advice from experts, you don't have to. This book is about coming to terms with a breakup and moving past it. It's about learning to stop thinking about him 24/7 and quit obsessing over the mistakes you made. (Rule Number One: Never promise a man a free trip to Fiji unless you really mean it.) It's about finding someone new—and finding yourself. Ultimately, it's about creating a new future.

Because believe it or not, you *will* get over him. And even better, you can take action to speed your own recovery. Sure, time heals all wounds—but that doesn't mean you have to sit around sobbing for six months. *Getting Over Him* will teach you how to take care of yourself immediately after the breakup and into the future, getting you through the pain with as little permanent scarring as possible.

How do you figure out what went wrong?

Introduction

What steps can you take to feel okay about yourself again? What do you say when he asks how you're doing? How do you quit obsessing over him? What are the most breakup-friendly tissue and waterproof mascara brands? *Getting Over Him* answers these questions and many more.

Think you're the only one who's ever felt this heartbroken? You'll soon discover you're not alone: This book is full of real breakup stories from real women just like you. It also features step-by-step advice from therapists, a quiz that tells you "How to Know If You Really Want Him Back or If You're Just Suffering from Sex-Deprivation Delirium," tips such as "Twenty Things You Could Be Doing Instead of Thinking about Him," and pointers on how to make your next relationship both healthier and happier. All in all, these pages deliver heaps of real help. The end of a relationship can feel like the end of the world, but *Getting Over Him* will show you how to overcome your heartbreak and find your way to a new beginning.

1

He's Out of Your Life—
And You're Out of Your Mind

The second after it happened, I was hysterically crying. My friend took me to Pizza Hut and I started throwing the silverware. I wanted to turn the table over.

—Diana, age 20

He made a point of doing all the things I love—taking me to a romantic dinner at a restaurant I wanted to go to, then to a jazz show, and finally back to my place, where he gave me a back massage. It was while I was giving him a massage that he dumped me out of the blue.

I was in shock. I started to cry. We sat down and discussed it a little, but after a while I felt stupid talking to him and sent him home. Then I curled up in my bed and cried for a month. And my friends will attest to that because they took turns baby-sitting me.

—Robin, age 24

He sent me a "Dear Jane" letter. I was eating dinner while reading it and immediately lost my appetite. I jumped in the shower and started bawling as the water and the tears all ran together. I was in there for almost an hour, until I was shriveled like a prune and out of tears.

After that, I didn't speak—not one word—for two months. If someone tried to talk to me, I would walk off. I wouldn't see friends. My family was totally freaked-out. It was like I shut down; I physically could not talk. All I could think about was the whole year Pat and I had been together, over and over—the good times, the bad, what went wrong, all of it. It was like a record skipping in my head that I couldn't shut off.

—Laura, age 25

I met Michael at school in Chicago. He was a real all-American guy, and every girl was after him. We dated for two years, and everything seemed perfect—he was my best friend as well as my boyfriend. When I decided to transfer to a college in another state, we agreed to have a long-distance relationship.

Once I got to school, Michael called me all the time, assuring me I was The One. Over Christmas break, he flew me to Chicago for a week so we could be together.

The first night I was there, Michael took me out to a romantic dinner at a fancy restaurant. Afterward, we went back to his place and he told me to stay in the foyer, then blindfolded me so I couldn't see him lighting candles all over the entire house. He took off all his clothes, turned out the lights, and removed my blindfold. Then we started kissing. We were really getting into it when, out of the blue, he started crying and fell to his knees. Then he said, "I can't do this. I'm gay."

I was in shock and didn't say anything. He was hysterical. I just hugged him and told him it was okay, not really believing what was happening. Then I left. I went over to my best friend's house and collapsed on her couch, sobbing. My world felt like it was crumbling, and everything I'd based my future on was a lie. I literally didn't get up from that couch for three days.

—Zanni, age 24

Right now you're taking the picture of him off your bedside table . . . and clutching it to your chest, removing the photo from its frame so you can get as close to him as possible. You're wondering if he ever really loved you. You're not only crying now; you're wailing. See, you've just been broken up with, and it hurts like hell. Just thinking about it pierces your heart with a pain so excruciating even George Clooney and his entire *ER* staff couldn't alleviate it.

Think you're freaking out? Don't worry, you're probably just reacting like anyone else would after a bad breakup. Chances are, you'll recognize many of the following symptoms. If you've been spared a few of them, count your blessings.

- Inability to concentrate
- Waiting for the phone to ring
- Thinking you see your ex on the street, at the dry cleaner's, in the grocery store, and then realizing it's not him after all

He's Out of Your Life

- Breaking out in tears every time you hear a love song
- Checking phone messages every five minutes
- Spending all your time daydreaming about your ex and trying to figure out how to get him back
- Dreaming about your ex
- Remembering the good times and forgetting the bad
- Wanting to ask mutual friends what he's up to, how he's doing
- Driving by his house or office
- Praying he'll come back into your life
- Losing track of your finances
- Feeling completely uninterested in other guys
- Losing your appetite or overeating
- Drinking too much
- Grinding your teeth at night
- Getting headaches, stomachaches, and backaches
- Suffering from insomnia
- Forgetting important things you need to get done
- Losing things
- Getting annoyed for no reason
- Feeling empty and directionless

Being in love is like being on a drug. Right now you're suffering from withdrawal, but you don't have to let your loss control your life. You *can* feel better. Here's how.

Dial-A-Friend

When your pain is still fresh, the natural temptation is to call him and patch things up. Makes sense, right? No, no, no! (Not yet, at least. We'll talk more about this in chapter 3.) Or perhaps you're tempted to lie in bed dissecting what happened. Also a bad idea! Although spending time alone reflecting on the breakup is important later on, it's the wrong move immediately after the fact.

Instead, phone your best friend, briefly explain what happened, and ask her if you can stay over at her place tonight. Then immediately remove yourself from the vicinity of the phone.

Why not just have your pal come over and stay with you? Because right now you don't need to be around the lamp you and your boyfriend bought together, the bed you shared, and that photo on your bedside table, okay? So throw a toothbrush and a change of clothes in a bag and get in the car. And as much as you might be tempted, do not take a scenic detour by his house.

When you get to your friend's place, let her take care of you. Imagine you're a sick child—that's the kind of attention you need right now. You'll feel better just being around someone else; after all, when you're feeling lonely, there's nothing worse than being alone.

And since she's your best friend, you can go ahead and wallow a little bit without feeling embarrassed or ashamed. Don't worry about being impolite or monopolizing the conversation or any of the other stuff you usually worry about with friends. Hey, your friend wants to help you—this is no time to ask her about the progress of her window-box radicchio. All social niceties are suspended in the face of this level of despair.

So sit down with her and go through every little minute detail of what happened—why he might have done such-and-such, what he could have meant when he said so-and-so. Be selfish and talk about you, him, and you and him. Get everything out and solicit your friend's assistance in analyzing it all, moment by moment. Between the two of you, eat all the ice cream she has in her freezer. Have a few glasses of wine. Cry. Stay up late if you want.

That's exactly what Darcy, age 23, did. "I went to my best friend's house and cried my eyes out. The only other people there were Ben and Jerry. We consumed two pints of Cherry Garcia and talked about what a jerk my ex was all night long."

At some point in the evening, however, you may want to give your friend a breather and vent to someone else. Are you very close to your mom? Your old college roommate? Maybe you want to talk to them about what happened, too. But don't get on the horn and tell everyone you send Christmas cards to yet; wait for things to become a bit more settled. For these first few days, it's best to let just close friends and family members know. "Reach out to a support network and talk about the experience," advises David Lutwin, D.S.W., a clinical social worker in private practice in Long Beach, New York. "Call people who can help you heal and go through the grieving process."

When all this outpouring of emotion finally exhausts you, it's time for bed. You may even want to ask your friend to sit with you until you fall asleep. Okay, you still feel bad. Awful, really. I wish I could tell you you'll feel all better tomorrow. But the truth is that you may feel even worse in the morning when you wake up and realize that your life with him is over, and you're facing a new day on your own. But don't worry; just as you got through today, so you'll get through tomorrow—and the day after that.

The Day After

If the following day is a Saturday or Sunday, either get your friend to do something with you for the day or call your sister or another close friend and plan to see her instead. Now is the time to contact people who care about you and can help you deal with the loss.

If, however, you're waking up on a weekday, call in sick. Hey, you probably do feel a little sick, don't you? Especially after all that Blue Nun and fudge ripple. . . . Face it: Trying to focus your mind on compiling reports at work would be a fruitless endeavor.

Your friend may offer to let you stay at her place for the day, but don't take her up on it. Otherwise you'll probably just end up sprawled on the couch watching back-to-back talk shows and thinking about jumping off a bridge. (Note: If you're *really* considering this, go to page 105, "He's Not Worth Dying Over.")

Instead of spending the day in tears, do some-

He's Out of Your Life

thing for yourself. Meet your mom or a pal for lunch, then catch a couple of matinees. For best results, stick to action flicks, horror films, or comedies—but no *romantic* comedies, natch. A movie allows you to lose yourself in someone else's story for a while; it's the perfect escape right now. You still get out of the house, but since you're anonymous in a darkened theater, you don't have to feel weird about going solo. Bonus: By going in the afternoon, you're likely to avoid those lovey-dovey couples holding hands and feeding popcorn to each other at the evening shows. "Seeing a movie was perfect," says Beth, age 24. "It got my mind off where I was and what was going on. Watching a story set in the big city took my mind away from all my problems in my little college town for a couple of hours."

While you're out, don't forget to stop by the drugstore to pick up a few necessary supplies for the long days and nights ahead: Puffs Plus with Aloe (to keep your nose from sustaining any more trauma than it has to), Visine (to make you appear as though you haven't been suffering from frequent crying jags and insomnia, even though you have), and Maybelline Waterproof Great Lash mascara (to ensure that your lashes look great—and smudge-free!—even through the tears).

Now you're ready to face going home. But that doesn't mean it's a good idea to be home alone. Call a couple of close friends, tell them what happened, and invite them over for dinner. A dinner party so soon? Yeah, right. Fear not; you're ordering takeout tonight.

Of course, if you share an apartment with your

ex and one of you hasn't moved out yet, a pizza pow-wow at your place might be impossible. After all, if he's crashed on the couch, you and your pals can't very well dis him in the dining room. For now, it's best to stay out of the home you shared as much as possible. Go to a friend's place instead. (For more information on this dilemma, see "When Your Ex Is Your Roommate," page 46.)

When your buddies ask you about the breakup, go through the whole process from last night all over again: Analyze and agonize until you feel you've covered all the major highlights (or lowlights) of the story. But afterward, join in when the conversation turns to other subjects. Tonight, you see, you make your first attempt at reentering the real world.

Which is good practice, because unless the next day's Saturday or Sunday—in which case you should hang out with friends again—you go back to work in the morning. You can't keep calling in sick forever, and besides, knowing you're getting behind at the office won't lower your stress level. So get up, already. (If you work with him, flip to page 37, where you'll find pointers on how to handle seeing him every weekday.)

Back on the Job

If you usually tune in to a pop-music or easy-listening radio station while you're getting ready in the morning, take a moment now to switch to a different frequency. Try news, classical music, heavy metal, talk shows, or anything else that doesn't feature tearjerker lost-love ballads every five minutes. Personally, I favored Nirvana CDs. Their music helped me get in touch with my anger and inner strength and made me feel better about my state of mind; even *I* wasn't as full of angst as Kurt Cobain was.

Now, before you leave the house, give yourself a little pep talk. Say to yourself, "I'm okay. I have my own life, and I'll be fine today." And believe it.

When you get to the office, tell everyone you're feeling a little better, but don't divulge the real reason for yesterday's absence. If you inform your boss and co-workers of your bad news, they may start to see your shaky mental state reflected in a decline in the quality of your performance—even if you're doing the same solid work you've always done. Instead, put on a brave face and do your job. At least that's eight hours out of the day you don't have to think about him. Do your best to keep it that way by concentrating on the tasks at hand rather than sitting at your desk calling all your pals—talking about him may only make you upset, and sobbing at your desk sort of mars your professional image.

Some additional things to try over the next few days (and beyond):

- Start keeping a journal. You can buy a beautifully bound blank book, or it can be just a spiral notebook. It doesn't matter, as long as you have a special place to vent all your feelings. Carry it with you at all times so you'll be able to write stuff down whenever it hits you. "After a while, you'll notice you have good days and bad days," says Sharyn Hillyer, M.F.T., a licensed marriage and family therapist in private practice in Los Angeles. "On a bad day, seeing that you've been there before and knowing what you did to make yourself feel better can help."

In addition to being a record of your feelings, your journal should also be a place for all your reconciliation schemes, all your apologies, all your accusations, all the questions you want to ask him, etc. That way, you'll have all your thoughts on the relationship in one place. This can be helpful later on, whether you're writing him a letter suggesting you get back together or trying to figure out exactly what went wrong.

- Get reminders of your ex out of your sight by putting away memorabilia from your relationship in a big box. His pictures and letters? Don't feel you have to look at them all again; just throw them in the box. The jewelry and sexy lingerie he gave you? Toss those in, too. Add anything that causes you pain just because you associate it with him—even if it's just the waffle iron he gave you for your birthday.

Once you've filled the box, you may be tempted to take it outside and set a match to it, or at the very least ceremoniously throw it into the nearest Dumpster. Don't. Later on, when the pain's subsided, you may want this stuff. There are a lot of memories in that box, and it doesn't make sense to literally throw them all away. Says Karrie, age 26, "When I now think, 'Why did I ever date that guy?' I look at my ex's old letters to prove to myself that there was a time he was nice to me. It reassures me that I wasn't a complete fool."

Instead, put the box in an out-of-the-way spot where you won't be tempted to get it out all the time. Try the attic, the garage, or the top shelf of your closet, behind your milk crate full of old magazines and underneath that pile of jeans with the holes in the knee that don't fit you anymore anyway. Or give the box to a trusted friend. After a few months, when you're feeling better and can actually enjoy its contents again, you can ask for it back.

- Eat right, do at least a little exercise, avoid drinking and smoking too much, and get a good eight hours of sleep a night. After all, the better you take care of yourself physically, the better you'll feel emotionally.
- Go on a shopping spree. Purchasing a pair of Italian pumps or a to-die-for cashmere sweater can be a great spirit-booster. "After my breakup, I went shopping and bought this little black dress I'd been eyeing for ages," says Alicia, age 20. "Buying something nice for myself made me feel happier and more attractive." Just make sure you don't go overboard—mountains of credit-card debt will only compound your stress level.
- Don't call him. He needs time and space right now, and so do you. There's a time to get in touch with him, but it's not quite yet. (More about this in chapter 2.)
- Try to maintain some perspective. Yes, you're longing for him. But you're strong, and you can live without him. These past few days are proof.

"When Ken left me, it really did feel like my heart was breaking," remembers Samantha, age

26. "But I'm an actress, and I just kept reminding myself to remember this awful feeling for my next role. When I win the Oscar, I'll thank my ex!"

If your life were a movie, so far you'd have gotten through only about a half hour. Are you going to walk out of the theater already? Give your life a chance to get exciting and climactic again. It will—promise!

Ten Videos to Lift Your Spirits

Speaking of movies... If you've got your ex on the brain, why not hit the video store for some cinematic diversions? These fantastic flicks are guaranteed to prove you're not the only one who's ever felt this way. When you're done, be kind, rewind—and then watch them again.

1. *Singles*. If the pain's so bad that you haven't seen daylight in a few days and the take-out containers are piling up, pop in this video and watch Campbell Scott suffer through the very same symptoms. Hey, guys feel pain, too: When Kyra Sedgwick dumps Scott, all he can do is lie on his couch—undressed, distressed, and depressed—and stare at the ceiling. Meanwhile, root for a newly confident Bridget Fonda as she blows off Matt Dillon's attempts to woo her back. The dazed look he delivers when it sinks in that she doesn't give a damn is worth a thousand late fees.

2. *How to Make an American Quilt*. If you're questioning the whole concept of men, marriage,

He's Out of Your Life   19

and monogamy these days, rent this movie and share Winona Ryder's life lessons on all of the above, courtesy of the anecdotal wisdom of her grandmother, her great-aunt, and their quilting-bee cohorts. In the end, she learns that mistakes in love are to be expected and forgiven. If only our mothers could be this objective! (Caution: Keep the Kleenex close by.)

3. *The Specialist.* If your vengeance fantasies include explosives and a clean getaway, may we remind you that while you can't get away with it, Sharon Stone can. Watch Stone get even for her parents' murders by seducing the mobster's son, then blowing the big guy's dynasty to bits. True, Stone is avenging a different kind of love loss here, but when she climbs into the driver's seat at the end of the movie, you'll feel better, too.

4. *While You Were Sleeping.* If you need to renew your faith that a sweet, lonely heart like yourself will find true love when you least expect it, check out this sleeper. Pay special attention when Bill Pullman demonstrates his "leaning in" theory on Sandra Bullock, and they fall clumsily all over each other on the ice. As you watch their chemistry practically melt the snow on the ground, you'll melt as well.

5. *Twenty-one.* If all your confidantes are out of town for the weekend, rent this movie and discover a new friend in Patsy Kensit as she looks straight into the camera and recounts her recent liaisons with a married man and a good-looking drug addict she can't help but

try to save. Her experiences as a smart woman who sometimes makes foolish choices will strike you as both funny and familiar.

6. *Swingers*. If you're looking for catharsis and comedy, this is the movie to rent. See the stunning Vince Vaughn et al. try to talk Jon Favreau out of the angst he's suffered since his girlfriend split up with him six months ago. Observe the torment answering machines have wrought upon Favreau's existence. And as you watch Favreau get back out there and try to play the game, remember that for you, too, there is hope.

7. *Cabin Fever*. If you're feeling totally sex deprived and don't know what to do with yourself, rent this soft-porn video written and directed by and for women. Basic no-plotter: Pretty, single artist is visited by a motorcycle-driving, leather jacket–wearing stud looking for carpentry work. Luckily for him (and her), she lives in a wood cabin. A sunken bath, roaring fire, and mosquito-netted bed star as the supporting cast. And best of all, you'll find this video in the drama section of the store, not the back room.

8. *He Said, She Said*. If you're in the mood to torture yourself with reconciliation fantasies, check this one out. Kevin Bacon and Elizabeth Perkins star as the impossible pair who keep coming back for more. Watch as they get off to a bumpy start, confess their love, move in, break up, and make up. When she tells him that all she wants to do is bash his "stupid, ugly, stupid face in," then tries to saw

his VCR in half, you'll be cheering her on. And by the end, you'll be cheering for them both.

9. *The Truth About Cats & Dogs*. If you're feeling especially vulnerable, who better to commiserate with than Janeane Garofalo in this romantic farce about a really cool chick (much like yourself, no?) who talks herself into feeling unworthy of a cute photographer's affections. It takes model neighbor Uma Thurman to help Garofalo appreciate her true beauty and uniqueness and realize that being herself is more than enough.

10. *Waiting to Exhale*. If you're feeling alone and unloved, this movie will remind you that though guys come and go, good girlfriends are forever. Laugh and cry right along with the four women leads as men do them wrong again and again; the dialogue, so true it hurts, will have you talking back to the TV like it will do them some good. Whenever you need to be reminded of the strength of girl power, this is the film for you.

The Eight Stages of Grief

You're no doubt going through a confusing whirlwind of emotions right now, and sometimes it's hard to know how to react. Feel lost? Read on for a little direction.

1. **DENIAL.** "This isn't happening to me," or "He'll call me any day now and tell me he wants me back."

How to cope: It's better to deal with the rejection than ignore it.

2. **SHAME.** "I feel like a failure," or "How can I tell my family and friends he left me?"

    How to cope: Blaming yourself is neither realistic nor productive, so cut it out. As far as your friends and family go, if they care about you, they'll understand. In fact, they're more likely to blame him.

3. **ISOLATION.** "I feel so alone," or "He's the only one who understands me."

    How to cope: You're not alone, and he's not the only one who understands you. Prove this to yourself by spending more time with close friends and family.

4. **ANGER.** "How could he do this to me?" or "If I see him, I'll kill him."

    How to cope: Your relationship didn't work out. That doesn't mean he hates you—or that you should hate him. You have a right to feel upset, but don't let it cloud your judgment or prevent you from learning from the breakup.

5. **BARGAINING.** "I'll lose fifteen pounds if he'll take me back," or "Please, God, I'll do anything to have him just call me."

    How to cope: Accept the fact that you can't change his mind for him, no matter what you do. And be aware that the promises you're making (to your ex or to God) may not be healthy.

6. **BLAME.** "I should have initiated sex more often," or "He ruined the relationship with his fear of commitment."

    How to cope: It takes two to make or break a relationship. Neither you nor he is com-

He's Out of Your Life

pletely responsible for its demise.

7. **DEPRESSION.** "I'll never love that way again," or "I'll never find someone."

   How to cope: Keep busy doing things for yourself to boost your confidence. And never say never.

Although you may go through the preceding stages in a different order, you'll eventually get to the final stage...

8. **ACCEPTANCE.** "It's over, and I'm okay," or "I can have a fulfilling life without my ex."

Why Breaking Up Isn't So Bad after All

In the long run, you may actually come to see your breakup as a blessing in disguise. Here are some reasons why:

- All those cute guys out there
- No more Sundays planned around the NFL schedule
- Partying with single friends you haven't hung out with in a while
- No longer having to waste the rest of your life waiting for him to make a serious commitment
- His back hair!
- Friends taking you out to dinner, calling you all the time, buying you little gifts to make you feel better
- The fact that he always seemed to conveniently "forget" his wallet on dates

- Anticipating the first kiss with a new hot man
- That annoying noise he always made when he laughed
- The freedom to do whatever you want whenever you want
- That ratty baseball cap he insisted on wearing (backward, no less)
- No more having to put up with his overbearing parents
- Becoming your own person again instead of just half of a couple
- Being able to throw out those ugly, gaudy earrings he gave you for your birthday
- Getting to fall in love all over again!

2

Getting Disconnected

You know you'd feel better if you could just contact him. After all, when something bad happens, he's always the first person you talk to. You want to tell him you're hurting. You want to know he's suffering; you want to know he still cares. You want to know he's home, regretting his decision, not out cavorting around town with some girl he met at a strip bar.

"I'd vow not to call him, but then I would do it anyway," admits Ivy, age 27. "It would feel so great just to be in contact with him. But inevitably, about an hour after we'd hung up, I'd feel even worse than before. It was like being on drugs—it's great while you're doing it, but then you need another hit."

As difficult as it might seem at the moment, it's probably best for you to stay away from him for a while. Getting in touch with your ex at this stage will only reopen the wounds from the breakup. (If you don't buy that theory, read on for horror stories from women who didn't keep their distance and lived to regret it.) If you must see him—either because you want your Picasso print back or because he sits in the cubicle next to yours at work—here you'll learn the skills needed to survive the sticky situation with style.

Look Who's Stalking

"I'd go by to see if he was home," says Virginia, age 26. "For some reason, I felt the need to see what he was up to. Of course, I didn't want him to know, so I had to do it secretly. I'd drive by really fast. Once I even dressed up all in black, hoping nobody would see me, and snuck around outside his house."

Another woman I spoke with used to work with her ex, so she knows his e-mail and voice mail access codes at the office. Months after the breakup, she still checks his messages daily.

Unfortunately, giving in to this kind of behavior only impedes your recovery. After all, it really doesn't matter what he's thinking or doing now. Since he's no longer your boyfriend, he's forfeited any further impact on your life. Besides, I hate to break this to you, but he's probably not spending all his time pining for you. "When it comes to breakups, you need to have as realistic a view as possible," advises Mick, age 25, who broke up with his girlfriend after four and a half years. "If it's over, it's over."

Bart, age 29, agrees. "If I've broken up with someone, I consider it to be final. Because it's so hard to break up, in the past I've postponed it until way beyond when I should have done it. It's hard to tell someone you don't want to see her anymore; you don't want to upset her. So you put it off. With my last breakup, I was ready to move on well before I initiated the split."

In order to understand why this is so often the case, you need to understand how a relationship ends. As Diane Vaughan writes in *Uncoupling: Turning Points in Intimate Relationships* (Oxford University Press, 1986), "Uncoupling begins with a secret. One of the partners starts to feel uncomfortable in the relationship. The world the two of them have built together no longer 'fits.' " Rest assured, it probably wasn't anything you said or did. Instead, it was more likely the realization of a deep-seated problem—a basic incompatibility between you, perhaps, or a fear of making a commitment. Whatever it was, suddenly he felt doubts.

Of course, you didn't hear about it when it happened. Although your ex may have felt frustrated, he may not even have known exactly why. In any case, he probably didn't communicate his frustration directly. Instead, it came through in subtle hints, such as sarcastic remarks about your dress sense, insults about your taste in music, or even the way he stopped kissing you hello when he met you for a date.

Eventually, his criticism probably became more pointed. Remember how he used to pressure you to go back to school? Or make jokes about your so-called low sex drive? Or complain about the fact that you refused to convert to his religion? In little ways you may not even have thought about, he was trying to change you to save the relationship.

However, although he didn't seem as lovey-dovey as he had once been, you didn't want to believe there was anything wrong. Even if you asked about it, he denied it. He was busy at work, or he was stressed out by something going on with his family. He said everything was fine. And he still told you he loved you; he still had sex with you; he still called you ... at least sometimes.

Unfortunately, he probably sent mixed signals, because he wanted you to be there until he was completely sure he wanted to go through with the split. In addition, he may have been attempting to soften the blow—however misguided that impulse may have been. Meanwhile, you were probably in a serious state of denial. To admit that there was a problem would have meant confronting the fact that your relationship—something that was probably a major part of your identity—could be breaking up. You didn't want to think about this, so you didn't.

In attempting to express his unhappiness, your ex began to focus more and more on the negative aspects of you and the relationship, which naturally didn't help matters. In fact, before long he was redefining not only your relationship's future, but also its past. He started thinking a lot about the fights you'd had; differences he had once brushed off now loomed large. There was trouble in paradise. However, he still didn't confront you with his reservations directly. He never said, "There's something bothering me about our relationship. This is what it is. Now, what do you

Getting Disconnected

think we should do about it?" Instead, he criticized you, even in front of others. Unbeknownst to you, he probably began to confide in close friends whom he thought would take his side. He also may have started seeing you less and hanging out more with friends you didn't know well, if at all. He started pursuing new interests. Slowly but surely, he was pulling away.

By this point, the relationship was essentially over—quite possibly before you even realized anything was wrong. See, when your ex's attempts to change you weren't successful, he started seeing the relationship as unworkable. And when he started communicating that to his friends, he was publicly dissociating from the relationship, subconsciously preparing to break up with you. In order to justify ending it, to himself and to others, he went over its problems again and again—which only served to deepen his resolve.

Mind you, none of this was done in a calculating way. On the contrary, he did it because he felt he had to. On some level, ending a relationship means admitting to failure. In order to accept that failure, your ex had to convince himself that he had no choice, that the relationship couldn't work. As he collected reasons not to stay with you, he was coming to terms with his loss and grieving the end of the relationship—even before it was over.

Because he put so much effort into interpreting your relationship negatively, he's not likely to change his mind. Although it may seem to you that the breakup was a sudden, rash decision, it's more likely that he'd been thinking about it for a long time. Chances are, there were problems with your relationship for a while, and it's only now that you're realizing it. He's already tried to "fix" things; in his eyes, it's probably too late. So what's the point of keeping tabs on him? Better to move on.

Call Waiting

No matter how badly you want to, don't call him. Yes, he's hurt you, and yes, you want him to know how much you miss him. But calling him isn't the answer. Unfortunately, a phone call from you at this point will only look desperate. If you want to tell him off, remember that indifference hurts more than harsh words ever could. And if you want to get back together with him, you're better off sitting down and writing him a letter (see chapter 3). If you make it too easy for him by rushing to ring him up even after he's done you wrong, you send the message that no matter how he behaves, you'll still be there, begging for more. Instead, do whatever you have to do to avoid dialing his digits.

"It got to the point where I would leave my apartment so I wouldn't pick up the phone and call him," says Ivy, age 27. "I would go see two or three movies in a row, visit friends for hours, sit in coffee shops—anything to keep myself out until late at night when it would be too pathetic to call. I know it sounds extreme, but it was only for a couple of weeks, until I got a handle on the situation. Besides, it worked. It's funny—the more time that goes by without contact, the less you crave it. It gets to a point where you realize that seeing or talking to him will actually make you feel worse, not better."

Make a pact with a friend that if you start to weaken, you'll phone her first to talk it over. Or delay your urge for a day: Every time you feel you must call him, wait one day. If you still want to do it tomorrow, then go ahead. That gives you time to think over what you're doing and decide whether you really want to go through with it or not. And don't cheat by calling him and hanging up "just because you wanted to hear his voice." News flash: He knows it's you. And he doesn't find it charming.

"A few months after the breakup, I called him just to hear his answering-machine greeting," says Julie, age 25. "I went to a pay phone so his caller ID wouldn't be able to trace the call. When the machine picked up, it was his new girlfriend leaving a message for a friend, saying to meet her and Jason at this place we always used to go. I felt like such a loser. Jason was out at our old place with his new girlfriend, and I was prank-calling him from a pay phone! I felt like a stalker. I went home really upset that night. It made me realize I needed to move on. He had a new life, while all I was doing was longing for our old one."

You may also feel compelled to go see him at his home or work. Trust me, banging on his front door or begging his secretary to let you see him will not jolt him into realizing his true love for you. If you have a problem keeping away, try substituting another behavior. Each time you're tempted to contact him, do fifty jumping jacks or rent a movie (go back to page 18 for rental suggestions) instead.

Same goes for dedicating songs to him on the radio or leaving notes on his car. The more you try to make your ex see how much you care, the more he'll want to pull away. "People usually want what they can't have," says Deborah Cooper, Ph.D., a marriage and family counselor in private practice in Los Angeles and author of the book *Understanding Your Lover* (Schaefer Publications, 1989) and the audiotape *How to Avoid Rejection* (Schaefer Publications, 1989). "Yes, it's sick and unfair, but it's reality."

Besides, consider the effect his response will have on you. If he's rude to you, you'll feel even more distraught. If he's nice, you'll torture yourself wondering if he wants you back. Either way, you can't win.

Can't We Be Friends?

Don't fall into the trap of thinking you have to remain friends if you ever hope to reconcile. In fact, if that's your goal, it's better not to pursue a friendship right away. If you're always friendly, always around, you may come off as desperate, not sweet. Take it from Robin, age 24: "I thought that he was scared and just needed to see that he couldn't find anyone quite as perfect for him as me, and as soon as he realized that, he'd come back to me. I believed that for a long time—six or seven months. I made sure I was still around and available to talk to. I tried to show him what a great friend I was. I tried to make him miss me.

"It was fruitless. He had started dating someone else right away, but he didn't tell me for a long time. When I found out, I was pretty angry, but there was very little I could do but scream and yell at him."

Jeffrey, age 24, agrees. "Tracy and I were friends, but I always felt like she was trying to start things up again. I never really questioned whether I could get together with her again; it was always my decision. I felt I had so much control that she would jump at anything I wanted and not think twice. That was bothersome, because it showed she had no individuality or backbone. You don't want to go out with someone who would do anything you say."

Likewise, if he's the one going out of his way to be buddy-buddy, don't think he's necessarily on his way back into your arms again. If he's handing you the "let's be friends" line, there could be several reasons:

- He's trying to let you down easy.
- He's keeping you on the back burner, just in case he ever changes his mind.
- He likes the positive reinforcement you give him—he knows you still care, and it pumps up his ego.
- He depends on you to help him out with money, family, or job problems.
- He wants to continue to have sex with you, even though you're no longer dating.
- He genuinely likes you as a person and wants to be your friend.

Even if you're sure his motivations are pure,

consider your own carefully. You may think you just want to be pals. And yes, eventually you can be. But can you really handle that right now? Karen E. Peterson, Ph.D., a licensed psychologist in private practice in Boston and author of *The Tomorrow Trap: Unlocking the Secrets of the Procrastination-Protection Syndrome* (Health Communications, 1996) and a forthcoming book on procrastination in relationships, points out, "Love minus sex doesn't equal friendship. Most people need a few months of healing and getting centered again before they can consider being friends with an ex."

So if he's contacting you and you want to keep him as a friend, tell him you need some time on your own right now, but you'll call him as soon as you feel ready. Of course, if he was abusive or didn't respect you, just tell him where to go; you don't need a "friend" like that. (See page 150 for more information on this subject.)

You should also back off from contact with his family and friends, at least for now. Sure, you like them, but continuing to phone them and hang out with them as if nothing ever happened will just prolong your pain. Ask yourself why you want to keep in touch with them. Is it because you want to maintain a connection with your ex? Is your bond based largely on the fact that you were both fond of him? If so, leave his loved ones behind; you'll be better off.

But if you honestly like, say, his sister—for who she is, not who she's related to—you can stay friends. Just give it time. If you call her right away, you'll probably be tempted to ask her for info: What does she think was really behind the breakup? What's he doing now? Is he seeing anyone new? Don't put her in this position; it's unfair to her and degrading to you. Instead, simply let her know that you need some time away from reminders of your ex, but that you'll call her just as soon as you feel comfortable. Then, after a couple of months—or however long it takes you to feel you can speak to her without making *him* the focus of the conversation—you can try resuming your friendship.

Oh No, That's Him

Naturally, at the exact moment you're finally getting used to being on your own again, you'll be guaranteed to run into him at the Laundromat. The scene: You're stuffing your last load in the machine when you do a double take. It's him, and he looks terrific. You, on the other hand, haven't showered yet, your cowlick's sticking up in this frankly rather unattractive way, and you're wearing a buffalo-plaid batwing-sleeved shirt and paisley jeans with ankle zippers from 1987—hey, all your other clothes are in the wash.

Hide! Just kidding. Instead, take a deep breath and simply tell yourself that you are so confident and naturally attractive that you don't need to doll yourself up every time you go out. Besides, you don't care what he thinks, remember? Okay, so it's unfortunate that you're feeling less than ravishing this morning, but don't pretend you don't see him. Instead, talk to him about his goldfish, the weather, the fact that there are never any dryers available at this Laundromat, and you don't know why you keep coming here. In other words, keep the conversation brief and on neutral ground.

Of course, you may also want to throw in a few factoids about how [fill in appropriate upbeat topic here] you just got a raise/you're going to Waikiki next week/you've been going out a lot and has he tried that wonderful new restaurant downtown? Whatever you chat about, be sure to be the first to say, "Well, it was nice running into you, but I've got to go meet someone. Ciao!" and then walk away. (Look, if your delicates aren't dry, you can pick them up later.) P.S. Follow the same general guidelines if you happen to see one of his friends.

When he sees that you are smiling, carefree, and (gasp!) actually living without him, he'll feel a bit perplexed. This doesn't quite jibe with his mental image of you sobbing over his old letters, sleeping with a photo of him under your pillow, listening to "your" song on CD repeat-play. Even if you *are* doing these things, he doesn't need to know. His thoughts: Whoa, she seems happy. And busy. And suddenly more attractive. Even if he doesn't want you back (or vice versa), you'll get major points for showing him that not only are you okay on your own, but in fact your life is a buzzing whirl of social excitement now that he's no longer in it. Which is far preferable to looking like a teary-eyed mess who can barely stand to look him in the eye, much less talk to him.

What if he's—uh-oh—with a girl? Leigh, age 25, has been there, seen that. "Right after we broke up, I saw my ex, Anthony, in a bar with another woman. My friends and I followed them to his place, and I got really upset. So the next night, I picked up some big blond guy, brought him to Anthony's favorite bar, and made out with him right in front of Anthony. Every time I ran into Anthony somewhere, I flirted with every guy to make him jealous. It was really unhealthy."

She's right. It is unhealthy. No matter how much you're tempted, don't stalk your ex. Or neck with hunks you hardly know, just to hurt him.

By the way, if you frequent the same club, buy breakfast at the same Dunkin Donuts or exercise at the same gym, it's best to start going somewhere else. Eventually you'll be able to go back to these places, but if you go too soon, it'll be hard not to remember times you went there together, when your relationship was still good. If you're reminded of him every time you go to the place where you're used to seeing him, you'll feel sad, whether you run into him or not.

On-the-Job Stress

"It was so hard to get over Robert because we worked in the same office," explains Dawn, age 30, "and I kept hoping that we would reconcile. Once, a few months after the breakup, we were both working super-late. I wanted to go out and do something, so I asked him if he'd like to get a beer. He said, 'Nope,' and that was it. No explanation, nothing. And then I had to see him again the next morning.

"The fact that we work together made me a lot more restrained than I might have been. I couldn't fly off the handle and become a screaming maniac. I had to remain dignified, so that meant sucking it up a lot."

If you work together, your breakup can be especially tough to handle. Instead of being able to move on with your life and get him out of your head, you're forced to see your ex eight hours a day, five days a week. It's not exactly easy to forget he exists when he's in the next cubicle.

Of course, one option is to quit and find another job. As drastic as that may sound, it could save you a lot of heartache in the long run. But if you don't want to do that, you'll just have to avoid him as much as possible: Don't hang out in his department, send him inter-office e-mails, or dine at his favorite lunch spot. And resist the urge to send yourself flowers to make him jealous. There's no point wasting your energy on him now.

This won't be easy; after all, you have a history. Be prepared for the memories that will inevitably creep into your brain during the 9-to-5 grind. "Walking down the hall that you used to kiss in after hours will be hard," warns Dr. Cooper. "But all you can do is stay away from him as much as possible. It's better not to see, hear, smell, or touch him. It will only kick you back into when you were still in love."

While you certainly shouldn't be buddy-buddy with him, it *is* important to be professional and polite. "When you do see him, be nice," advises Dr. Cooper. "There's no reason to be a bitch." If you're forced to work with him directly, obviously you'll have to spend time with each other, but your interaction should still remain strictly business—which means no discussing weekend plans, whom you're seeing, or any other aspect of your personal life, past or present. Unfortunately, however, he may not be as considerate. If he's being rude to you or overly nosy about things that have nothing to do with work, tell him you realize it's an awkward situation for both of you, but you'd rather keep your conversation to a minimum. If he tries to engage you in an argument over it, just calmly say, "I don't want to discuss this."

If he seems intent on making your work life difficult, "you could always say, 'I think it would be best for us to be civil when we see each other,'" advises Dr. Cooper. "You might also tell him that you think it's not a good idea for either of you to flaunt new dates around the office." You should both understand that having future romantic interests pick you up from the office for lunch or after-work drinks doesn't make it easy for anyone.

Being the topic of conversation around the watercooler may be another concern. If co-workers didn't know you were dating, don't tell them now. But if the relationship was common knowledge, keep the explanation of your split short and sweet. As Suzanne Lopez, M.S., M.F.C.C., a psychotherapist in private practice in Los Angeles, advises, "Tell your co-workers as little as possible. Instead, deal with the breakup in friendships outside your work arena. If people ask, just say, 'We're no longer together, and I'd rather not talk about it.'" You may think telling your co-workers about all the ways he's wronged you will make him look bad, but more likely it will just make you seem petty and unbusinesslike.

If you report to your ex, this adjustment will be doubly difficult. "When the breakup involves you and your boss, he's probably not going to leave," says Lopez. "You're going to have to ask for a transfer, or you'll have to go." Of course, you can always try to stick it out, but taking orders from the man who used to take your breath away isn't easy. See how it goes. If he's ultracritical of your job performance or you feel you're being unfairly treated, try discussing it with him in a nonaccusatory way. If, after you hash it out, his behavior still doesn't change, consider reporting him to his superior or to Human Resources. They may agree to talk to him or arrange to transfer you to a different department. But before you go above your boss's head, check your employee manual: Some places forbid employees to date, and you could wind up getting both you and your boss fired.

If your ex reports to you, you'll have to deal with a lot of these same issues. "If you're his boss," says Dr. Cooper, "try to set it up so you're not seeing each other too much. Do everything possible to maintain a friendly breakup so it doesn't pour over into the work performance. Build up his self-confidence. Expressing anger isn't going to be appropriate." The best way to handle dealings with your ex is with the utmost professionalism. Any hostility or harsh criticism can be construed as harrassment and grounds for complaint.

Since you're the higher-up in this case, you don't want to jeopardize your position. But, at the same time, says Dr. Cooper, "you can't control him. You can't make him quit. *You* can quit if you want—or choose to deal with the pain." Which is not to suggest that you can't use your influence to help out both of you. Pull some strings and see if you can secretly recommend your ex for a job elsewhere. When he gets a call recruiting him for a position at another company, he'll probably jump at the opportunity, especially given the situation. Sure, you're doing him a favor, but by getting him out of your hair, you're doing yourself a favor, too.

Finally, let this experience be a lesson to you: Don't get involved with someone you work with. The reality is that most relationships eventually break up—and, as you now know, dealing with the aftermath for forty hours a week is no picnic. Don't put yourself through it again.

Many Happy Returns

Unfortunately, he still has your Conway Twitty album, your Frisbee, your college sweatshirt, your SaladShooter, your humidifier, your three ice-cube trays, and your toothbrush. And well, doggone it, you want them back.

Chances are, he wants his stuff, too, though he might not always get it. Some women see refusing to return a man's belongings as a reward for their heartache: "He had this Cure T-shirt, and I wanted to keep it," says Janice, age 24. "It's so huge, it makes great pajamas. Besides, there was no way I was giving back his favorite shirt."

But this works both ways: If you don't give, you probably won't receive. "He didn't get his stuff back, but I didn't, either. He still has a pair of my gloves and a few of my T-shirts," says Dawn, age 30. "In fact, some of those shirts still appear on him. The first time I saw one, I was like, 'Nice shirt.' He just ignored me."

Avoid your own personal Shirt Wars by simply returning his things and requesting yours. Obviously, this means a temporary suspension of the no-contact rule. Compose yourself by holding off for a week or so before getting in touch with him, but don't postpone it too long or he may "lose" your stuff, claim he never had it, or give it away. While you're waiting, make a list of everything you left behind: You don't want to have to bother him again when you realize you forgot to fetch your felt fedora on your way out the door.

Likewise, start putting his junk in a box. Don't wear his wool socks or brew tea in his kettle—you don't want his things around. Personally, I made the mistake of using James's big-enough-for-two umbrella. I'd given it to him for Christmas a year and a half before the breakup, and together we'd huddled under it during many walks in the rain while we lived in London. Since he'd left it in my closet when he moved back to Sydney, I would grab it on cloudy mornings, and every time I got it out, I remembered our good times. After the split, the umbrella started to take on symbolic meaning, representing a time when we walked arm-in-arm through every thunderstorm.

Then one afternoon I left it in a movie theater. As I walked out, I took one look at the near-monsoon conditions that had developed over the last ninety minutes and dashed back in to retrieve it. Alas, by the time I realized what I was missing, someone had snatched it. So I went back out into the cold, windy wetness alone, with nothing and no one to protect me. By the time I managed to hail a cab, I was not only soaked, I was crying.

Often we cling to objects he's left behind because they're all we have to hang on to. When you write with his fountain pen or light his candles or make recipes from his cookbooks, you feel a connection to him again. It brings back good memories. But it also helps keep you hooked, which is another good reason to give back each other's stuff as pronto as possible.

Don't hold on to his things as a way of holding on to your relationship. Even if he tells you to hang on to his stuff for a while, don't listen. The implication is that he'll return, so you figure you'll just keep his croquet set until you reconcile. However, if you want him back, you'd be better advised to return his belongings and ask him for yours as soon as possible. Don't let him get away with putting you on hold: Let him know that if he needs a little breathing room, you're giving it to him. And in the meantime, you don't need his cleats clogging up your closet.

If you call him and he claims he doesn't want his stuff (or if he just stopped calling one day or skipped town without informing you), get rid of everything by selling it or giving it away to friends or charity. As you remove his possessions one by one from your apartment, you'll feel your attachment to him weaken: Somehow, you're not just getting rid of his belongings, you're getting rid of *him*. If he out-and-out denies he has anything of yours (though you know better) or simply refuses to give any of it back, consider whether the stuff he has of yours is worth more to you than the stuff you have of his. If so, you could always consider small-claims court. But as long as you didn't lend him your Rolls-Royce, it's probably wiser to let it go rather than prolong contact with a guy who is obviously a jerk.

But say you can't handle seeing him right now regardless. In that case, arrange to mail each other your things or get a sibling or friend to handle the exchange for you. Otherwise, call him (yes, this means a brief suspension of the no-contact rule) and set up a time to drop by his house. The biggest advantage of going to his turf is that if he "forgets" to give you back your CD collection, you can collect your tunes then and there without having to arrange another meeting or just cutting your losses. Plus, you have the added bonus of walking out and slamming the door on him and your old life—a nice image to leave him with.

Once you have a time set up, call a chum and ask if she's up for a movie, your treat. The catch? She gets the opportunity to sharpen her chaperoning skills during a pit stop to your ex's place. See, your pal's presence guarantees you won't have a big fight or hop in the sack with him on a whim, and the movie date assures that you look like a girl on the go ("We've got to run—the Ralph Fiennes flick starts in fifteen.").

Here's the plan: Wear something casual and comfortable, not slinky and sexy—you want to look good, but not like you're trying to impress. Toss all his stuff in a cardboard box—no sweet I-hope-we-can-be-friends Hallmark card, no satin ribbons around his old magazines—and go pick

Getting Disconnected

up your pal. Go to the theater nearest his house and purchase the movie tickets, preferably for a film he would have never, ever have accompanied you to. That way, you're giving your visit a definite deadline and showing him you have your own interests, thankyouverymuch.

Drive to his place, blasting girl-empowering tunes like Helen Reddy's "I Am Woman" or Alanis Morrisette's "You Oughta Know" along the way. Then knock on his door, best bud in tow, and remind him you're there to get your stuff. Plaster a pleasant look on your face and say a few words of greeting. If you must get into a conversation, bring your friend into the conversation as much as possible ("Jessica just got back from Jamaica!"). This way, the focus isn't entirely on you and your precarious feelings. When you exchange goods, check to make sure yours are all there, and ask him to do the same. Then tell him you have flick tix and have to run—fact is, while he's sitting around in his apartment doing nothing, you've got plans. Finally, shut his door with a smile and speed straight to the Cineplex. After all, you don't want to miss the previews.

If, however, he says he hasn't gotten around to gathering up your stuff yet (despite his agreement to do so by now), he's obviously pulling a passive-aggressive move by deliberately making things difficult for you. Maybe he wants you to come back later—alone—so he can try to get you into bed, or maybe he figures he'll get his things back but never have to give back yours. Or maybe he's just really lazy and will never get it together enough to gather your belongings. Whatever the case, forfeit your movie date and enlist your friend to help you collect your things from his apartment now (promising to really, really make it up to her later). If you wait, you may never see your possessions again—and chances are, they're worth more to you than fifteen dollars' worth of movie tickets.

When Your Ex Is Your Roommate

You shared love, life, and living arrangements. But now that you're no longer an item, what happens next?

If he's the one moving out, stay at a friend's house for a few days. This should allow him plenty of time to get his stuff out, but just to be sure, give him a concrete deadline via voice mail, e-mail, or note; it's best not to talk to him directly at this stage. Once his move-out deadline has passed, it's time to reclaim your once-shared territory and make it your own. Just to be on the safe side, change your locks immediately. And while you're at it, consider changing your phone number, e-mail address, and answering-machine access code (no need to be his secretary for the duration of the lease). Once that's out of the way, overhaul the place. Paint the walls your favorite color (or one he always hated)—passion pink, maybe, or chartreuse. Get a puppy. Hang a disco ball. The place is yours now, so you can do whatever you want.

If you're the one changing addresses, move your stuff out as quickly as possible. The sooner you move out, the sooner you can move on. If you're not ready to find a place yet, put your belongings in storage and stay with friends or family for a while. Moving straight into a new place, especially if you'll be living alone, can be a bit overwhelming—but it has been done. Just proceed with caution, and don't be afraid to ask friends and family for emotional support.

Whatever you do, don't try to continue living together after the breakup. It's impossible to heal when he's in the same room, and seeing each other on a daily basis will cause both of you heartache, as Melissa, age 33, can testify. "When Luke and I broke up, we waited until our lease expired to move out. Three long months. It was a big, big mistake. I don't know what we were thinking—it was really foolish."

No matter what the circumstances of your breakup, continuing to live with him afterward is a bad idea. But when your breakup was difficult, it can spell disaster. Jacqueline, age 32: "After Andrew and I broke up because I found out he was cheating on me, my new apartment wasn't available for three or four weeks. So in the interim, I moved up to the attic of his house. It was a nightly torment. During the day I felt strong, but almost every night after work I went out with my friends and got drunk. At least two or three times a week, Andrew and I got into a big confrontation. And we ended up sleeping together on a few occasions; at the time, I felt I was getting something over on the other woman, but in the end *I* was the one being used. Living together afterward draws out the agony of a failed relationship—you really have to make a clean break."

If you lived together, it can be especially difficult to split the goods, since there are probably things you bought together. Make a list of joint items and decide before you talk to him what you want and what you don't. That way, when you do discuss it, you won't become so overwhelmed that you blurt out, "Oh, you just take it all." (Later on, when you're entertaining guests on the floor of your new apartment because you gave *him* the couch and matching recliner, you may regret it.) If you know in advance what you're fighting for, you're more likely to negotiate for at least a good part of what you deserve.

Even if you don't have shared possessions, moving out can get messy. Sometimes it's the little things you struggle with, as Jenni, age 25, notes. "My breakup with Brian was awful. I figured he would throw a fit over me taking what was rightfully mine, so I had to be sneaky about claiming my goods. While I knew he was at a friend's house, I got ten people to come over, and we moved all my things out in an hour. I left him with nothing except the stuff that was originally his—an ashtray, a blanket, his TV, and the phone. I even took the toilet paper, but then I started to feel guilty, so I went back and left him a little."

As it happens, though, Jenni's ex had an even more fastidious sense of detail. She explains, "Not long after I moved out, I got a call at work about some things that had gotten packed with my stuff by accident. It was the police. The guy said, 'This is Officer So-And-So, and I have a formal complaint here that you have stolen ten pairs of boxers, twelve pairs of socks, fourteen T-shirts, and two books.' Even the officer thought it was ridiculous."

But if you're lucky, claiming your possessions

can end up being less traumatic than you expect. Ivy, age 27: "The night my ex broke up with me, I just left, so I had to go get my stuff over three or four lunch-hour cab excursions. I didn't want him to be there when I came back because I didn't want to put him out. That, and I didn't want him to see me. I'd never been broken up with before, and I felt pathetic, embarrassed.

"Anyway, the last of these trips was during the week before Christmas. I got into the cab and the driver looked exactly like Santa Claus—it was eerie. As we drove downtown, I was crying to the point where I was getting dry heaves, I was so upset. He asked me what was wrong, so I explained what had happened. When we got to my old building, this man backed the cab up to the front door and went into the apartment to help me get all my stuff and pile it in the trunk.

"As we drove across town to my new apartment, I was crying harder than ever, so the driver started telling me about his wife of forty years, and how I'd know when it was right, and how this guy didn't sound like he was the one for me. Then he helped me move my stuff into my new place. When we were done, he wouldn't let me pay him. He took my hand in both of his and said, 'In twenty years you're not going to remember that guy's name, but you'll remember me.' It was just what I needed."

Ex Sex

If your ex wants to get lucky after the split, tell him to try a casino. "Sex after the breakup only complicates things," says Rick, age 25, who broke up with his ex after three years. "It's usually a woman's attempt to get a shred of something back." His advice? "Keep your dignity!"

Jeffrey, age 24, agrees. "My ex-girlfriend would set up situations where we'd have one-night stands. This happened three times. Once she came over and brought a bottle of wine, which we drank in my room. Another time, we went out to a movie as friends, went to a bar, and then she came back to my place and basically said she would spend the night. In the end, I had no respect for her."

"My ex wanted us to continue to sleep together after I broke up with her," says Bart, age 29. "I had a hunch she wanted to get back together, but sex wasn't going to affect my decision. I think guys have the ability to separate the physical from the mental. I could have kept fooling around with her and still felt in my mind that we were one hundred percent broken-up. But I knew that wasn't the right thing to do, so I didn't do it—except sometimes, you know, when I was really loaded."

As a marriage and family therapist, Sharyn Hillyer sees this same scenario over and over again. "So often we think we're going to lock him in with the sex, but a lot of times a guy is just taking advantage of what's offered to him," she warns. "I wouldn't sleep with him unless you had a real commitment. You should agree to sex only if he's giving indications that he wants to work things out and that the two of you are going to work on the relationship and make it different." In other words, his calling at three A.M. saying he misses you and wants to come crawl into bed with you doesn't count. If he really wants to get back together, he ought to ask you to sit down and discuss it with him—outside of the bedroom.

True, some women can go to bed with an ex after the breakup, enjoy the physical act, and get on with their lives. Some even report that it makes them feel back on top (so to speak). "All the chemistry came back instantaneously," says Dawn, age 30. "But I wasn't like, 'I missed you so much.' I wasn't as expressive or emotive as I had been in the past. It was more like getting caught up in the moment—he was just a guy to me. The next day, I felt more at ease than I had in so long. I felt the scales balanced again."

But chances are, you'll have an experience more like 23-year-old Lana's. "Two months after the breakup, he called to say he wanted to be friends and didn't want me out of his life. I told him, 'I need time and space right now, and if you want me in your life, it has to be as your girlfriend. We are not Jerry and Elaine on *Seinfeld*!' I told him I couldn't turn the relationship back and just be friends with him."

Unfortunately, however, Lana's feelings ended up winning out over her resolve. "Of course I really missed him, so I did eventually try to be his friend. I thought if we were friends, he would eventually want me back. I stayed at his place one weekend, and we had sex. I thought this was a good sign, but afterward he apologized and said it had been wonderful, but it was a mistake—it didn't mean anything."

Lana's story is a perfect example of why "postbreakup sex is a very, very bad idea," according to Kathleen Mojas, Ph.D., a clinical psychologist in private practice in Beverly Hills. "It's usually a desperate attempt to get that old feeling back or hook the guy again: You think, 'If I sleep with him now, then I'll feel this connection and gratification and do away with any insecurity or anxiety I'm having about the end of the relationship.' It's not an expression of love and caring, and it doesn't mean the problems in the relationship are solved—it just means you're now reconnecting to a guy you should be disconnecting from."

In fact, sex with an ex hardly ever has a happy ending, whether or not you wish you were back together. Perhaps you're considering it because you think one last fling with him will give you some sort of closure and allow you to get on with your life. Not likely! In fact, since sex tends to strengthen the bond between lovers (especially for women), it can end up making it more difficult than ever to let go. Once he gets dressed and walks out the door, you'll feel the rejection of the initial breakup all over again—even if you honestly don't wish he were back in your life.

Besides, no matter how good the sex was while you were dating, it won't be the same after the breakup; you'll probably find yourself experiencing too many conflicting emotions to actually relax and enjoy it. "We fooled around a couple of times after we broke up, but both times I felt awful afterward, like I was being used," remembers Julie, age 25. "The second time, I pushed him off in the middle. I was like, 'I don't want to do this.' He said, 'Are you tired?' I thought, 'Yeah, tired of you.'"

The point here is that you don't need him—for

sex or anything else. Besides, as Dr. Mojas reminds us, "It's not like we can't help ourselves. You've got a right hand."

The Suddenly Invisible Man

What do you do if you haven't even officially broken up? If your relationship ended with a disappearing act—that is, your boyfriend stopped calling you altogether or moved without so much as a forwarding zip code—it's time to escape your love limbo and face the inevitable.

"I had dated one guy for two months when he told me he was going on vacation to Belgium for a few weeks," remembers Virginia, age 26. "But a month later, he still hadn't returned. I was very confused and wondered what the heck was going on. Then someone told me he had moved there! I still don't know the full story."

A similar thing happened to Missy, age 27. Although her boyfriend didn't move to another continent, he might as well have. "Jon gradually blew me off. He would never call me and would always break plans, but he wouldn't break up with me, either. We started seeing each other only once a month, and I noticed he put his pictures of me in his underwear drawer. But when I'd ask if we were splitting up, he'd say, 'No, I just need some time. I'm just going through a phase.'"

Missy knew that Jon had recently been through a difficult divorce, so she tried to be understanding. "I gave him some space, but this continued for three months. I didn't even get a three-second call from him on my birthday. He didn't want a breakup scene, so he tried to make it end by non-communication."

Finally, Missy couldn't stand it anymore and decided to confront him. "It took me a very long time to pin him down. After we finally set a time to meet, he left a message on my machine saying his roommate had gotten tickets to a Phillies game, so he was going to go to that instead. But when I called him a week later and asked him how the game was, he said he hadn't even gone."

Finally, they set another date. "This time, Jon didn't cancel, for once. I went to his house with this twenty-page letter I'd written when I was worried I'd never see him again. When I got to his place, his roommate was there and he had a friend over, so they were all hanging out. Finally his friend left, so we went outside. Jon said, 'Okay, I'm ready—go ahead and yell at me.' I started talking about everything, telling him he hurt me when he didn't want to talk to me and asking why he felt he had to conquer his problems on his own. He heard everything I said, but showed no emotion. His response was, 'I'm no good for you. I don't deserve to have happiness.' There was no way I was changing his mind about our breakup, but I felt better saying everything that I wanted to get off my chest and telling him I thought he should get counseling.

"After we talked for a couple of hours, he said he had to go to work. I was crying, so he said, 'Oh, it's not that sad. We can still be friends.' I thought, 'Yeah, right.' When he walked me to my car, I handed him the letter I'd written him. That was the first time I could see any recognition on his face that this really did mean a lot to me. He was like, 'I can't believe you wrote all this.... Don't worry, everything will be okay.' I haven't seen him since. But at least I knew we were broken up."

See, it's impossible to get on with your life when you and Mr. David Copperfield are still technically together. If your soon-to-be ex is available, you need to officially break it off, preferably in person. Let him know he's hurt you, calmly ask for an explanation for his behavior—you deserve that much, at least—and say good-bye for good.

If there is absolutely no way of reaching him, you need to accept the fact that it's over on your own. Write him a "Dear John" letter and send it to his last known address or his parents' house; with luck, it will eventually be forwarded to him. Or have a "funeral" for him: Invite a couple of close friends, grieve over your relationship a little, and bury a photo of you and your ex together. And while you're at it, bury any hopes that he's coming back. Odds are, he's not.

Getting over someone who didn't even have the courage or consideration to officially break up with you is especially difficult. Not only do you have to deal with the fact that he's no longer in your life, but you also get the added bonus of wondering: a) Is he coming back?, b) What the hell happened?, and c) Are we broken up yet? To save you some time and trouble, the answers to those questions are: a) Probably not, b) You may never know, and c) Most definitely. Time to move on.

3

What If You Want Him Back?

You were so in love! You're perfect for each other! He's going through a tough time right now, but you're destined to be together!

At least, that's how I felt. When James and I broke up, I really thought we'd get back together. Oh, sure, the separation hurt all the same, but at least I had the consolation of believing it was only temporary. He was young. He wanted to experience life on his own, be independent, date other women. As soon as he'd gotten that out of his system, we'd be back to being "as close as pale blue and light sky blue" (yes, he actually wrote that in one of his letters). Wouldn't we?

He sent me letters telling me his news and saying he missed me. Saying he still thought about me all the time. Saying he still loved me. I was patient. He had been the one to end the relationship, and he would have to be the one to ask for me back. But on my twenty-seventh birthday,

What If You Want Him Back?

over a year after we'd broken up, he called me, and I couldn't stop myself.

"James," I heard myself saying, "I got your last letter. What's going on?"

"What do you mean?" he asked.

I hesitated. "Well, your letters make it sound like you want to get back together with me. Is that right?"

"Well, maybe someday," he said. Those things he wrote in the letters? They were true, he said—he still did have really strong feelings for me. But he wasn't ready to act on them yet. He just wanted to wait and see.

I pointed out that it had been two and a half years since we'd been together on a day-to-day basis, and over a year since we'd broken up, yet he was still saying the same old things. "How much time do you need?" I asked. "I think subconsciously you're just trying to keep me on the back burner in case you ever change your mind." I was crying now, softly, dabbing my nose with a tissue, trying not to let him hear.

"No, it's not like that," he said, his voice calm and soothing. "I just wanted to let you know that there's someone out there who really cares about you. I was just being honest about my feelings."

"Okay," I said. "I guess I misinterpreted things. But now I understand. I guess now I know what you're really thinking...." At this point I started to sob, partly because I was so upset but maybe partly because I wanted to make him feel guilty and show me he still cared.

"Don't cry," he said. "I didn't mean to hurt you."

"I love you, James," I said, tears streaming down my face.

"I love you, too."

But that's when I knew it was really and truly over. I had waited, and waited, and waited some more. I had dated other guys, sure, but never taken any of them seriously. In my heart, I was still waiting for James, but it was on that day that I knew I couldn't wait any longer. I got off the phone feeling really empty and sad and tired inside. Some birthday.

Do You Even Want Him?

When your boyfriend says he doesn't want to be with you anymore, it hurts. You know this; you're living this. But when you hang on to the relationship even after he tells you it's over, you're hurting yourself. (Believe me, I know.) So before you get your heart set on getting him back, keep the following "don'ts" in mind:

- Don't count on a reconciliation because you're looking for a way to escape the pain you're in now or because of your fear of being alone in the future. If you and your boyfriend broke up, there was probably something really wrong with your relationship, whether you realize it or not. After all, if he was the one for you, you'd still be together, right?

And just because you no longer have a fulfilling relationship with your ex doesn't mean you can no longer have a fulfilling relationship period. In fact, your future relationships will probably be even better because of all you'll have learned from this one.

- Don't fall into the trap of thinking that you've invested so much time and so much of yourself in your relationship that you shouldn't let it go. Melissa, age 33: "I was forcing Luke to be The One. Clearly, there were problems and big differences between us, but I rationalized them and convinced myself that I could deal with them. I had invested so much time in him, and in us, that I thought that was all life had to offer me."

  Don't make the same mistake. As Dr. Peterson cautions, "That's like saying, 'I spent two hundred thousand dollars on this house, put in a new floor, remodeled all the bathrooms, and added full landscaping—but we had a hurricane last week and the place is devastated. And now the builder says the foundation is unstable, and it'll never be safe again.' Am I going to continue to live there, or am I going to move on?"

- Don't look for "signs" that your relationship will get back on track. I used to think James and I were meant to get back together because I had dreams about him all the time. Obviously, however, this line of reasoning isn't exactly sound. Instead of thinking my dreams were an omen, I should have seen them for what they really were—my subconscious working through my grief.

  Ivy, age 27, also says she's seen a so-called sign: "I was watching *Mad About You*, and it turned out to be a rerun that I'd never seen. It was all about how Paul and Jamie met. Basically, it was fate—they met at the dry cleaner's, but then Paul had to track Jamie down. Which is exactly how Nat and I met. We were both waiting for our clothes at a dry cleaner's-slash-Laundromat, so we started talking about what we were reading. The conversation lasted for no more than five minutes, and we didn't even exchange names. It took him a long time to find me. I'd told him where I worked, so he basically called everyone at the company and asked if there was a girl from Florida working there, until he reached me.

"Although we broke up after four years, I'd always thought Nat and I would get back together—even after he got engaged. I still think there's more to come with us. And watching that *Mad About You* episode just made me think: Why did they pick this way for the couple to meet? I think what the show was saying was that there are soul mates, and that there is such a thing as fate. Paul and Jamie are supposed to be the perfect couple, which is what I'd always believed Nat and I were, too. I felt like calling Nat and asking him, 'Did you see that?' I figured even if he was home watching that episode with his fiancée, he would have to be thinking the same thing I was. I don't know why I can't just let it go."

On a strictly logical level, Ivy probably realizes that TV programs aren't carrying special messages meant just for her. When you want something badly enough, however, your mind plays tricks on you, assigning grave importance to random, trivial stuff like seeing his cousin's car pass you on the interstate or hearing "your" song playing the second you turn on the radio—things that actually have nothing whatsoever to do with you or your relationship with your ex. Next time you think you see an omen, try to keep that in mind.

- Don't listen to friends who chime, "Don't worry, he'll come back!" every time you bring up the breakup. Chances are, they aren't being objective—or realistic. They probably just don't know what to say or how to comfort you, so they tell you the only thing they can think of to make you feel better. In the short term, their predictions do reassure you, but in the long run, they'll just prevent you from moving forward.
- Don't think that the fact that you still have strong feelings for this person necessarily means you can overcome whatever problems you were having in your relationship. It's only natural to long for your lost love now; this tends to be true almost regardless of the quality of the former relationship. For instance, you could love someone who treated you badly or shared very few of your interests—but that doesn't mean you ought to rekindle your romance.

Pay attention to your priorities: "Make a list of things you're looking for in your relationships—with your friends, your family, and a boyfriend," says Dr. Peterson. "This could include anything from good communication skills to an interest in boating. Then look at the qualities you'd like to get from a man—which shouldn't be everything on your list—and ask yourself how many of these things you were getting from your boyfriend. If you weren't getting ninety percent or more, ask yourself if the missing ten percent was minor or major. If it was minor, fine, but if intellectual stimulation is really important to you, and he'd rather watch football, that might well outweigh everything on your list." Listen to your mind, not your heart, here. You may look back on your breakup and realize he did you a favor.

So before you get down on your knees and beg for his return, stop and think: Do you really want him back? If you're still not sure, take the following quiz.

How to Know If You Really Want Him Back or If You're Just Suffering from Sex-Deprivation Delirium

1. How did he refer to you when he talked about you with others?
    a. the love of my life
    b. my girlfriend
    c. the woman I'm dating right now
    d. my friend
    e. this girl I know

2. You see your ex as:
    a. your best friend
    b. worth holding on to—he may be the best you'll do

What If You Want Him Back? 63

    c. an investment—you've already spent so much time getting to know him and planning your future together, you don't want to have to start over with someone new
    d. confused about his priorities right now, but it's nothing that a little marriage and family couldn't take care of

3. Whenever you talked to your ex about things such as what you liked about your favorite brand of cereal or what your boss said to the head of the shipping department that afternoon, he:

    a. was riveted and asked for more details
    b. listened with at least a semblance of interest
    c. had to stifle a yawn
    d. often interrupted you to the point that you felt you had to fight to be heard

4. When the two of you talked, you found:

    a. you often had nothing to say
    b. your mind frequently wandered
    c. your interests and beliefs were very different from his
    d. you learned new things about each other every day
    e. you trusted him enough to share all your secrets

5. When you asked to meet his friends and family, he:

    a. claimed they all live in Greenland

GETTING OVER HIM

    b. tended to change the subject
    c. suggested you have dinner at his parents' and go out with his best buddies for drinks that very weekend

6. When you were around your own friends or family, you often felt:
    a. proud to call him your boyfriend
    b. embarrassed by his behavior

7. The one who always seemed to give more to (and want more) from the relationship was:
    a. him
    b. you
    c. neither one—you were equally involved

8. You only realized that he was your one true love after he broke up with you:
    a. true
    b. false

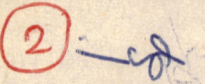

9. You knew you could trust him:
    a. always—you'd be shocked if he ever lied to you; you value his judgment
    b. some of the time—but you found you had to forgive him more than you'd like
    c. never—you've noticed a pattern of irresponsible behavior; you wouldn't trust him to water your begonias over the weekend

10. He and his family:
    a. are as close as the Cleavers

What If You Want Him Back? 65

b. get along fine, as far as you know
c. haven't seen or talked to each other in several years
d. are constantly feuding

11. You would describe him as:
    a. a loner—he doesn't really have any good friends except you
    b. popular—everyone loves him
    c. the type of guy who has a few very close friends he hangs out with a lot

12. He used to say "I love you":
    a. often—both in special moments and out of the blue
    b. rarely—only in bed or whenever you were really down
    c. never—he always said it should be obvious he cared or he wouldn't be with you

13. Your family and good friends:
    a. love this man and think you're perfect together
    b. think he's a great guy and everything, but not right for you
    c. tell you to watch out

14. This guy reminds you a lot of:
    a. one of your best friends or someone you've always admired
    b. all the other exes who broke your heart
    c. the parent who never seemed to have time for you when you were growing up
    d. a pal you like but see only now and again

15. When you were with him, you:
    a. loved spending time with him
    b. knew he was going to leave you
    c. were afraid he was using you
    d. fought all the time

16. In your final breakup scene, he:
    a. seemed conflicted and sad
    b. acted detached and relieved
    c. screamed a lot and said he never wanted to see you again
    d. well, actually, there wasn't one—he just stopped calling one day and you haven't seen him since

17. Since the breakup, he's:
    a. called you nightly as if you never even broke up
    b. told you that you mean a lot to him and that he'll always be there for you as a friend
    c. been totally out of touch with you
    d. spread rumors about your performance in bed

18. While he was in a relationship with you, he (choose all that apply):
    a. often talked about his ex
    b. always seemed to hold back a little, never allowing himself to become fully involved in the relationship
    c. insisted that holidays and birthdays were conspiracies created by card companies
    d. cheated on you

What If You Want Him Back? 67

- e. made you feel that nothing you did was ever quite good enough for him
- f. told you he had problems with commitment
- g. often made plans with you and then broke them
- h. would regularly shower you with gifts, tell you how much you meant to him, and then not call you for several days
- i. tried to control you
- j. was good to you only as long as you put out
- k. criticized you more than he complimented you
- l. could make a commitment to you, but not to your future
- m. repeatedly betrayed your trust
- n. was married to someone else
- o. abused you
- p. told you he'd discovered he's gay

Scoring

1. The way he referred to you says a lot about how he felt about you. Did he take the relationship seriously or treat it (and you) like no big deal? Sure, Shakespeare claimed a rose by any other name would smell as sweet. But hey, even the greatest playwright in history couldn't be right all the time.
a = 2, b = 1, c = 0, d = −1, e = −2

2. Your relationship should be based on your feelings for him, not your fear of being alone.

If you're not confident he's The One, you owe it to yourself—and him—to keep looking. Ditto if he doesn't feel the same way about you. Isn't being on your own preferable to being locked into a mediocre relationship?
a = 2, b = −1, c = −1, d = −2

3. You want a man who cares about your day-to-day existence; after the honeymoon period, that's what a long-lasting relationship is all about. If hanging out together meant one or both of you often becoming a bit bored, forget it. Things like good looks and sexual chemistry aren't as important in the long run as a genuine interest in each other's life stories.
a = 2, b = 1, c = −1, d = −2

4. Being able to talk easily and share your lives with each other is the foundation of a good relationship. If you don't trust him, feel he understands you, or really enjoy talking to him, what do you expect will keep the two of you together?
a, b, or c = −2, d or e = 2

5. A man who doesn't want you to meet people who are important to him is either hiding something or placing very little value on your relationship. If you want to be his leading lady, you have to meet the supporting cast, right?
a = −2, b = −1, c = 2

What If You Want Him Back? 69

6. You should feel comfortable with your boyfriend in social situations and want to show him off. Did you avoid going out with him in groups or doing things as a couple with your family? If you were often afraid of what he'd say or do next, maybe you weren't as well suited as you thought.
a = 2, b = −2

7. Relationships that suffer from a definite one-up, one-down power dynamic are usually doomed. Although you may have had periods where you felt more or less in control, those times should roughly even out. Even if you were the one who always seemed less interested in the relationship, don't think your sudden change of heart means everything is now hunky-dory. (See next question.)
a or b = −2, c = 2

8. Remember, rejection is the greatest aphrodisiac; your feelings now are not completely trustworthy. It's too easy to want what you don't have. Is he going to have to periodically threaten to leave you to keep you convinced that hey, maybe you really do value this relationship after all?
a = −2, b = 2

9. Without trust, there can be no real love. If he's a bad boy who rebels by lying, cheating, or generally disrespecting you, you deserve someone more mature. Your boyfriend

should be someone you know you can count on.
a = 2, b = −1, c = −2

10. A man who is close to his family has been taught from an early age how to relate well to others. Which would include you. That saying about watching how a man treats his mother to see how he'll probably end up treating you *isn't* just an old wives' tale.
a = 2, b = 1, c or d = −2

11. If others don't value his company, why should you? He doesn't have to be Mr. Popular, but if he never hung out with anyone else, that should give you cause for pause. Do you really want someone who depends on you for every bit of his social life?
a = −2, b = 2, c = 2

12. A man who is incapable of communicating his feelings isn't worth it. If he can't seem to get the L word out of his mouth, it's time to get him out of your life—for good. P.S. Sorry, but answering your "I love yous" with "Ditto" only cuts it if your boyfriend is Rush Limbaugh or the fictional character Patrick Swayze played in *Ghost*.
a = 2, b = 1, c = −2

13. When Mom and Dad tell you he's not good enough for you, don't automatically assume they're being overprotective. And when your friends warn you about him, try to keep an

What If You Want Him Back?

open mind. Of course, you ultimately have to make your own decision, but sometimes your loved ones can be more objective about what's good for you than you can.

a = 2, b = −1, c = −2

14. Your boyfriend should be someone you'd want as a friend, even if he weren't your lover. If he reminds you of someone else who hurt you, it's not a good sign. Likewise, if you were just whiling away time with him, look for a guy you can feel closer to.

    a = 2, b or c = −2, d = −1

15. If you were too busy worrying about the relationship to relax and enjoy each other's company, what's the point? Questioning his motives, anticipating his departure, or constantly feuding doesn't leave much room for fun.

    a = 2, b, c or d = −2

16. Unless he feels a little heartbroken, too, there's not much chance of a reconciliation. If he's happier without you (or if he just took off), in the long run you'll be happier without him, too. You want someone who wants you; if *he* doesn't, you can find someone who *will*.

    a = 2, b = −1, c or d = −2

17. How he's acting since the breakup tells you a lot about what he's feeling now that you're apart. If he's trying to maintain some type of a relationship with you, it doesn't necessarily

mean he wants to get back together, but it does improve the chances.
a = 2, b = 1, c = −1, d = −2

18. These are all indications of an unhealthy relationship. Subtract 2 for each letter circled. If you circled m, n, o, or p, don't bother adding up your score: You shouldn't even consider rekindling your relationship. Rejoice that you're no longer seeing someone who will never be available to you, takes advantage of you, or physically harms you.

What Your Score Means

Between 17 and 34: Star-Crossed Lovers

You loved each other a lot, but there may have been some fundamental problems. Can these be overcome? Think seriously about your needs before contacting him, and realize that you both have to want this to make it happen. Maybe things could work out between you. But the truth is, they may very well not. After all, a breakup is an indication of something having gone seriously wrong in your relationship. Fixing that could take a lot of work—and it's work you can't do just on your own.

Between 16 and −16: Well, It Was Nice While It Lasted

Chances are, your ex was fun to date, cared about you, and could be quite a romantic. But in the end, you want to build a future with Mr. Right, not Mr. Pretty-Good-Sometimes. You're hurting now because you're lonely, and you're afraid you'll never meet your best match. But you know what? This guy's no substitute for the real thing. Shed some tears, sure, but don't overromanticize this affair. Looking back, you probably could have seen it coming. Next time, you may want to steer clear in the first place.

Between −17 and −58: Quick, Run the Other Way

Something's amiss here. That you're heartbroken over a man who took advantage of your trust and treated you like a passing interest says more about you than him or the doomed relationship. Forget the loser. Develop your own interests, focus on your career, and work on building stronger relationships with your friends and family in order to give yourself a greater sense of self-worth and a vision for your future. After all, why would you want a relationship with someone who treated you this poorly? Are you happier with *anyone* than alone? Spend some time thinking over why you might be tempted to continue a relationship that's going nowhere. And if this feeling of desolation continues, give counseling (see page 169) a try.

Trying to Get Him Back

So you've thought about your relationship, and you're still convinced that you and your ex belong together. Now what? Let him know you're interested (carefully).

First, some things *not* to say:

- "But you promised me we'd be together forever."

    Maybe he did. But he hasn't fallen on his head and gotten amnesia. He knows what he said. And though repeating it to him might make him feel guilty, it won't make him snap his fingers, exclaim, "Oh, yeah, that's right!" and plead for your forgiveness.
- "I can't live without you!"

    Yes, you can. Saying you can't makes you look desperate and needy. Besides, who wants to be with someone who depends on a man for her happiness?
- "I'd do anything to have you back."

    Offering to adjust your behavior or personality to his specifications is not only pathetic, it's a huge turnoff. You're saying you have no respect for yourself; only *he* matters. You deserve someone who likes you for *you*, not who he wants you to be.
- "Look, if you want to get back together with me, you'd better decide by December first."

    Unfortunately, ultimatums will make him feel resentful, not romantic.

"The more you try to push yourself in his face, the more he'll resist," says Dr. Peterson. "If you want to be in his mind, the best way is not to be in his physical presence." This is especially true if he got out of your relationship because he had problems committing. "Never chase a distancer—it'll just make him create even more distance. But that doesn't mean you have to wait and see what he does, either. In fact, some men might be too proud to call after breaking up with you, so you'll have to be the one to contact him.

"You don't want to be demanding, but there's a difference between that and being assertive," Peterson continues. "You put what you want out there on the table, and see if he'll pick up on it and meet you halfway."

Here's how Dr. Peterson recommends finessing it:

1. As soon as you've decided you want to try again (whether this is the day after the breakup or a few weeks later), write down everything you'd like to say to him—how he's a jerk for treating you so badly, how you loathe those ugly green high-tops he always wears, how you long to shake him and demand that he realize how good he had it. Get out all your anger and frustrations. If you want, tell him you hate him and can't believe he would do this to you. Obviously, that won't make him want to drop everything to be with you, but it will allow you to get those feelings out of your system. Besides, you're not going to mail this. It's just for you.

2. Then write a letter to him. Tell him what you feel, what you think you did wrong, and what you would like to see change about the relationship. Express yourself calmly and clearly, without being accusatory or letting emotions

get in the way. "You may even want to try writing with your nondominant hand [that is, your left if you're right-handed]," says Dr. Peterson. "That can help you tap into the nondominant part of your mind and get feelings out that you might not have even known were there. You'll probably have to write slowly, but you may find that it unblocks you." Worried that your letter looks like it was penned by a six-year-old? Don't worry; you won't be sending this one, either.

3. Edit what you've written and think about how much you actually want to say to him. Which parts of your letter are truly constructive? Leave those sections in and ditch the rest.

Do you tell him that you no longer want him to put his family before you? Cut that sentence. This may well be an issue you need to work on if you do get back together, but reading that now will only put him on the defensive and push him further away. You can bring it up later, in person, if and when you *both* decide to iron out your differences. Do you spend a whole paragraph talking about how much you miss him? Toss it. You're already going out of your way to contact him. The fact that you really miss him is obvious, and even if you feel a little desperate, you don't want to show it.

Try to approach what you're writing from a position of confidence and strength. Even if you feel weak, he doesn't have to know. After all, the advantage of sending a letter is that you can precisely control the content; on the phone, it's too easy to let emotions flare up, which can obscure the message you're trying to get across.

You'll end up writing several letters before you finally have one you're ready to send. And though you've penned pages upon pages by now, the finished product should be fairly brief. "You might even want to send just a short note," says Dr. Peterson. "Something like: 'Dear Sam, I'm glad we talked and that we were realistic about breaking it off before things got worse. I won't be contacting you because I want to give you the space you said you need. I hope I'm still available if you want to work this out later. As you know, I still love you and am thinking of you. Love, Sally.'"

If you want to say more, talk about what you thought was worthwhile about the relationship, but admit where you fell short on your end: Maybe you didn't listen well enough, or maybe you were too critical of him. You certainly shouldn't go out of your way to highlight your shortcomings, but if you feel guilty about something you did or didn't do, now's the time to get it off your chest. It's hard to confess your own faults, but if you do have regrets, admitting them can open the lines of communication.

For example, you could say, "We had a very honest relationship, and that means a lot to me. I always felt we could tell each other anything. But at the same time, I now realize that I should have let some things go instead of nagging you as much as I did. Although I only did it because I care about you, in hindsight I can see how it must have hurt you, and I'm sorry." Then ask if you can get together and talk things over.

That leaves the door open for him to make a move. This is key. You've put the ball in his court, but he's got to run with it. Remember, you shouldn't have to convince him. "You know you're a good woman and a catch," Dr. Peterson says. "If you have to keep reminding someone of that, think of what that does to your self-esteem."

Dr. Mojas agrees. "Why would you want to talk someone into being with you? You deserve to be with someone who adores you and thinks you're great. Otherwise, you'll always feel a sense of insecurity."

If He's Stringing You Along

Sometimes, even after you're broken up, he'll act like you aren't. He'll ask you to dinner, send you witty e-mails, call just to say hi. For a woman who wants to get back together, this can be mighty confusing. Does he want you back, too?

Maybe—but then again, maybe not. Proceed with caution. Take it from Bart, age 29: "When I broke up with Tasha, there was a period of a few months where she maybe didn't think we were as broken up as I did. As far as I was concerned, it was final. But we were part of the same circle of friends and would often end up at the same places. We'd still hang out together, and I was fine with that because I liked her as a person and enjoyed her company, but I wanted to draw the line. However, she still wanted to be my girlfriend, and it was difficult sometimes. I could look at a social situation and say, 'This is my friend Tasha—we're going to do something together.' But in her mind, she might have been thinking, 'This is my ex, Bart, who I want to get back together with.' Was I leading her on? It's tricky."

Moral of the story: Mixed signals might not mean a thing. Noelle, age 25, learned that from experience. "Evan and I met when we were in Prague on a fellowship together. There was an instant connection, and we dated the entire time we were there. Our relationship was extremely intense, and we were almost never apart. We both had significant others back in the States, but we had made agreements with them to date around while we were apart. Obviously, it was difficult for Evan and me when we came back because we lived in different cities, and we both had people waiting for us back home. Although I almost instantaneously broke up with my old boyfriend and moved to Seattle, Evan stayed with his girlfriend in D.C.

"Still, we kept in pretty close contact. Evan would call and tell me that things between him and his girlfriend weren't good and that he totally missed me. At the same time, I was writing these passionate love letters to him, spilling all my feelings. He didn't encourage it, but he didn't *discourage* it, either. We talked on the phone for hours every few weeks and continued to write back and forth for a year.

"One day, I decided to fly out and show up on his doorstep. When he answered the door, I pretty much jumped him. It turned out that his girlfriend was out of town for the weekend; I couldn't believe my luck. I pushed him down on his bed and went in for the attack. His girlfriend didn't believe in premarital sex—meanwhile, premarital sex with him was all I could think about! But he said, 'No. I can't betray my girlfriend.' I was like, 'But your girlfriend doesn't care about you—*I* care about you. *I* want to be your girlfriend.' He refused to give in, saying he couldn't do that to her. This, after I'd flown thousands of miles and heard about their problems and how much he missed me for an entire year.

"After that, we basically just sat on the bed looking at each other. The scene was pretty charged and awkward. At one point, in this rather manipulative way, I said, 'If we only kiss once, it will alleviate the tension.' We did kiss, but he stopped before it went much further. Then he said he didn't want to sleep in the same room with me. Since he only had a studio apartment, he slept in the closet.

"Once he closed the closet door, I sat there, mortified. I was humiliated that I had come on to someone else's boyfriend. And I was so aggressive—not that there's anything wrong with that, but it was pretty extreme. I was also angry at him. The whole year we had been writing letters, I guess he thought it was more of a game, this little secret from his girlfriend. To me, it was very real—I was thinking that this was the person I wanted to spend the next five decades with. I would say, 'I want to get back together,' and mean it, but he would reply, 'Yeah, I miss you, too.' It was all hypothetical to him.

"When I left the next morning, we both seemed

confused. It was obvious Evan was more into his girlfriend than he had led me to believe. For a year, I had held on to something that was in actuality nothing like the glorified image I had built up in my mind. We never saw each other again."

If you fear your ex is stringing you along, don't let it continue. If you want to get back together with him, you should have made your wishes known by now by sending him a letter. Unless he responded to that by saying—that's right, *saying*, not *implying*—that he wants to get back together, you need to break off contact with him immediately. Remember, this doesn't mean you'll never speak to him again. Eventually, when you can handle it (see page 201), you'll be able to be friends with him again if you want. But this limbo stage does nobody any good.

If he says he can't decide if he wants you back, tell him to call you when he knows for sure—but don't wait by the phone, either. You might think that being the understanding, at-his-beck-and-call ex-girlfriend will make him realize how much he really loves you and can't live without you. But in reality, your hanging around just confirms that he can have you back whenever he wants you. And how can he respect someone who's waiting in the wings and putting her life on hold just in case he decides he wants her back?

Learning to Let Go

Once you realize that you can't control how he feels or what he does, you're free to think about yourself and concentrate on your own well-being.

"Letting go is hard, but when you realize you're powerless over the end of a relationship, it's much easier than trying to control the situation," says Joan E. Childs, L.C.S.W., a clinical social worker in private practice in Hollandale, Florida, and author of *The Myth of the Maiden: On Being a Woman* (Health Communications, 1995). Sitting by the phone "just in case he calls" won't help. If he really wants you back, he'll leave a message or phone again. Stay busy; pursue your own interests (see chapter 6). A break from each other will allow you to get more in touch with who you are and what you want—and help you gain insight into how and why you and your ex started moving in different directions.

Granted, your boyfriend might come back, but if he does, it'll probably happen only after you've given up on him. Just ask Jennifer, age 30. "Steve and I dated for two months the first time. I had really fallen for him. But he was going to law school out of state the next year and having second thoughts about getting involved. He didn't want to have a long-distance relationship, so we ended it."

Steve, age 29, remembers: "Our breakup was unemotional and more businesslike on my end. I was finishing college and moving on, and it seemed like we were through. I think maybe she was a little more attached than I was. I guess it wasn't the same on both sides."

A month after they broke it off, Jennifer invited him over for dinner. "I wanted to prove to myself that I could see him and just be natural and not try to hook up with him. If he did think of me, I wanted him to remember me that way instead of as the person on the phone saying, 'You're wrong about us; you need me,' as I had done right after the breakup. I wanted to leave that independent image in his mind."

On that note, she didn't quite succeed. "I don't recall us having dinner after the breakup," says Steve. "But I do remember that she didn't ever really make an effort to get back together. If she had called trying to get back with me, I may not have gone along with it. I was trying to put the past behind me and start fresh, dating other girls and hanging around a new circle of people. But Jennifer and I had mutual friends, and her name would come up occasionally. That got me thinking about her again."

Jennifer feels her nonaction prompted Steve to reconsider their relationship. "I think not hanging on to him and giving him some space helped. I thought if it's meant to be, it's meant to be. But when he called me a year later, I was leery. He hadn't seen me for a year, and now he'd decided I was the one for him? That seemed strange to me. I didn't trust him right away."

Steve could understand Jennifer's trepidation. "When I first made the call, it was more like a casual, 'what the hell' kind of thing. But Jennifer didn't want me to come back, sweep her off her feet, and then be done with her again," he recalls. "I had to be serious in order to see her. She wanted to hear all these committal things at the outset—that I wanted to commit, I missed her, and the timing was right. But it wasn't until I heard myself say those things to her that I knew I was ready."

Things were much different the second time

around. "I was able to set some of the guidelines because I wasn't so smitten," Jennifer says. "By the time he came back, I had enough self-confidence to know I could live without him. That made our relationship a lot more healthy. And now we're happily married."

What does Jennifer see as the secret to her success? "The key thing was that I had been over him for a long time before he called back. The more you get on with your life, the more the other person has to respect you."

So don't call him. And if he calls you, tell him you're busy and explain that unless he wants to talk about getting back together, you simply can't speak to him right now. In fact, it's best not to talk to him at all until he's either ready to get into a relationship with you again or you're ready to accept that you're going to be just friends now, period. You must not let him take you for granted. "If he knows he can come running back to you anytime he wants, then he's not going to get a chance to miss you, and that's what he may need," says Dr. Peterson. "If you're at his beck and call, that's the best of both worlds in his eyes." You become his consolation prize in case single life doesn't work out. However, if you make it clear that although you still care, you're getting on with your life, he may reconsider. "How often do we hear stories about how as soon as a woman is seeing someone else or becomes unavailable, her boyfriend comes back?"

Treat your relationship with your ex as if it were over for good. In fact, once you've written your I'd-like-to-try-again letter, try to forget him. Although you could continue to plan your life around "What if?", why would you want to? Letting yourself waste time hoping for a reconciliation keeps you in pain, prevents you from healing, and squanders energy you could be using to nourish new relationships or work on your existing ones with family and friends.

Above all, protect yourself. If you're finding it difficult to move on, imagine that your emotional pain is physical pain instead. If there's a brick wall in front of you, does it make sense to keep running into it in hopes that it might fall down? How much blood are you going to shed before you stop consciously hurting yourself?

Stacey, age 18, regrets not letting go sooner. "I tried to get back into the relationship countless times. I called my ex on the phone constantly but then would start to cry when I'd hear his voice. I'd plead with him to give me another chance. I'd lie and tell him I needed to return some stuff to him, just so I could see him. I sat at home and waited for him to call, hoping he'd decide he wanted to see me. I wrote letters upon letters to him and even gave him pictures of us together, hoping they would spark a memory. But all these attempts at reconciliation failed.

"My mistake here was not walking away when it was over. But he was my first love—the person I shared my first kiss, my virginity, my feelings, and my heart with. To think he didn't want me anymore made me feel worthless inside. And so I just kept holding on, setting myself up for hurt time and time again.

"I turned Jeremy into this perfect boyfriend in my mind. But that wasn't how it was. He made me miserable a lot of the time, too. In the end, it wasn't really Jeremy that I couldn't let go of; it was the secure feeling of the relationship. He used to be my best friend. We did everything together. That's what was so hard—knowing he could live without me and be happy."

Don't let this happen to you. If he doesn't respond to your letter, walk away with your head held high. You've given him the choice and done all you can. If he lets you go, you know it's his loss.

If He Cheated On You

"Ned and I met at work," said Lacy, age 24. "We were nineteen and in love, planning to get married the following year. But then I started hearing from other friends who worked with us that Ned had slept with another coworker, Mary. When I confronted him about it, he confessed and admitted he wanted to see other people. I was shocked and told him it would be better if we weren't together anymore.

"It was an awful situation, especially since we all worked at the same place. And, to make matters worse, Mary wasn't that great-looking, so I thought: If he likes her, what does that say about me? I hated seeing them together. They would be all lovey-dovey right in front of me, her wearing these spandex miniskirts and hanging all over Ned. It was an embarrassing slap in the face. I definitely wanted to quit, but I didn't want to let them think they had broken me.

"After a week and a half, Ned realized he'd made a mistake and told me he wanted to get back together. We talked a lot about why he had cheated in the first place; he said he had been scared about getting married so young and had been looking for that last fling. He realized that he had really hurt me and that it would take me a long time to trust him again. Even though his affair devastated me, I still loved him. Over time, we managed to iron out our differences, and now we're married."

As Lacy's story illustrates, the question of whether or not to get back together with your ex becomes even more complex if he cheated on you. You're probably feeling rejected, angry, confused, disgusted, hurt, or all of the above over the fact that he was with another woman behind your back. However, while you previously may have been a big fan of the "if you stray, you pay" philosophy, the situation often gets less black-and-white when you're actually living it. You might still love the guy and want to believe it will never happen again; he may seem deeply regretful, begging your forgiveness. But before you even consider ushering him back into your arms, you need to do some serious soul-searching. Here are five points to consider:

- Think about your relationship as a whole. Were you happy most of the time, or was it a constant uphill battle? If it's the latter, cut your losses and move on. Without a strong past, it's difficult to build a strong future.
- Decide whether he's worth trusting again. Has he lied to you before? A guy who has a history of dishonesty is more likely to deceive again than someone who's always been trustworthy

in the past. If your boyfriend constantly lied in your relationship, not only about major things (like supposedly shooting pool with his best buddy when he was actually with another woman) but also about minor points (like the story that he was once offered a high-paying executive position at work but chose not to take it), how can you believe the promises of infinite fidelity he's giving you now?

- Pay attention to his actions as well as his words. If you're open to the idea of getting back together and he's swearing he'll be faithful forevermore, make a mental note of what he's saying and see if he lives up to his promises during the next few months. Earning your trust again shouldn't be automatic.
- Consider whether he's up to the challenge of the changes that he needs to make. Is he willing to examine why he cheated on you and take responsibility for his contribution to the problems in your relationship? If not, the chances of you making it work are slim. Unless he learns from his mistakes and makes some positive changes, he's likely to stray again.
- Ask yourself what you're really looking for. Do you want him back because you really love him, or just because you miss the comforts of being part of a couple? Remember, it's hard work to rebuild a relationship crushed by infidelity. If you miss having a boyfriend instead of having *your* boyfriend, save everyone a lot of time and trouble and move on.

If you do decide to get back together, be prepared. The reconciliation road isn't always a smooth one. Even after you patch things up, there may still be some difficulties. "It's hard to trust Ned, even now. At times, we're never happier," says Lacy. "Yet at other times it's difficult to see why we're still together. You think that as time goes by you would forgive and forget, but it's much easier said than done. We try hard to be honest with each other, but I don't know if I will ever trust him as much as I did before he cheated.

"My advice to a woman in the same situation? Look inside yourself and see if it's the actual person you want back or the companionship. I really missed Ned when he was with Mary, but on many levels I just didn't want to be by myself. We've managed to make it work, but it's been a long, hard process. Just know what's ahead of you and then decide if it's worth it."

If You Cheated On Him

"I had been dating Jeremy for two years when I started developing a crush on a guy I met through work," says Stacey, age 18. "Jeremy and I were having problems at the time, so that just made it easier to fall for Darrin. He was there for me as a friend and offered me a shoulder to cry on when I needed one. One night, Darrin came over after I'd had a fight with Jeremy. I was crying and upset, and we ended up kissing and fooling around. We didn't have sex, but it definitely changed everything.

"The guilt was so hard for me to handle. I

guess I cheated because neither Jeremy nor I was happy. He never hit me or anything, but he yelled at me a lot, which didn't do much for my self-esteem. I felt that cheating on him was my way to hurt him like he had hurt me. He had his suspicions about it, so I confessed and we broke up.

"After a few weeks, I decided Jeremy was everything to me and I couldn't see my life without him in it, so I ended things with Darrin and tried to win Jeremy back. I had to regain his trust, and that was a very hard thing to do. It took a lot of late-night talks, but we honestly felt that we were better together than we were were apart."

If you cheated on him, convincing him to get back together with you is a tricky proposition. First, consider the points in "If He Cheated on You" and put yourself in his shoes. Then read the following guidelines:

- Be patient. His trust has been betrayed, and a simple "I'm sorry" won't restore it in a heartbeat. Expect him to be skeptical.
- Keep your promises. While you may really mean it when you swear it'll never happen again, he's probably not putting much stock into what you tell him at the moment. Following through on your word is the only way to make him believe what you say.
- Think long and hard about what made you stray. Discuss the problems in your relationship, and own up to your part in them. Work on making changes so you won't be tempted to cheat again. (See page 165 for more on breaking bad patterns.)

- Evaluate why you want to get back together. Is it a real reconciliation or just a Band-Aid for your guilty conscience? If it's the latter, leave him out of it and talk to a trusted friend or get into therapy to deal with your guilt instead.

Stacey offers these final words of advice: "The main thing to remember is that if you do get back together, don't cheat again. I broke my promise and went back to Darrin during the times things weren't right with Jeremy. When the truth came out, I had to tell Jeremy I had been with Darrin on and off for some time. If you need to cheat, something is wrong in the relationship, bottom line. If you don't fix it, it will just happen again. That was the case with me and Jeremy, and we ended up breaking up for good. At the time, I was devastated and tried everything to get him back again. But finally I realized it just wasn't meant to be."

If He Does Come Back

"Derek and I met in college, and there was always a strong attraction between us," remembers Ashley, age 25. "Although he had a serious girlfriend back home, they had an agreement that they could see other people. I really liked him, so there were lots of times we would meet up at a bar and end up going back to my place and kissing in the living room or whatever.

"Everyone knew I was so into him—my roommates used to tease me about following him around like a puppy dog. But after a few months, I told him I couldn't take the fact that he wasn't treating what was between us like a real relationship. He basically looked at me and said, 'I can't really give you what you want. I do have a girlfriend.' So we stopped seeing each other.

"I felt like I had lost the love of my life. It was terrible. But after our conversation, I knew I had to put physical distance between us. I pretty much stopped going to the bar we always went to. If I did go and he showed up, I'd leave. I didn't call him. I filled my calendar with going out with my roommates."

A couple of months later, Derek broke up with his girlfriend, but by that time, Ashley was dating someone else. "I think Derek thought I was going to get right back into things with him, but in my heart, I had really written him off. Even after I broke up with my new boyfriend, I still kept my distance. I just wasn't ready." Several months later, Ashley sent Derek a letter explaining what she thought had gone wrong between them and the way she wanted to be treated.

When she saw him in class the following Monday morning, Derek suggested that they leave early and get breakfast. While they ate, they discussed the letter, and he explained his side of the story.

"We really talked things out," Ashley recalls, "and I ended up inviting him to my sorority formal. Then, as we walked out of breakfast, he said, 'Do you want to go see a movie tomorrow night?' He told me he would borrow a friend's car and pick me up and do everything right. If he hadn't done that, sure, we still would have gone to the formal, and it would have been fun and all, but that would have been the end of it. Instead, he was making an effort. It was a second chance for us.

"He knew I wasn't happy with the way he'd been treating me, so once we were back together, he did things totally the right way. We took it slow, and he proved himself to me again and again. He'd walk me back to my place and wouldn't even try to kiss me or anything. He was a real gentleman. For example, one weekend after we started dating again, we ran into each other at the bar we always used to hook up in, and he said, 'I don't feel comfortable being in this setting anymore. Let's go somewhere and grab a hot chocolate.'

"At the same time, I didn't make it easy for him. It wasn't even that I was scheming—it was just that I had been through so much and had been burned by him before. We both changed a little bit. I stopped coming on as strongly as I used to, and he started treating me the way I'd always wanted. We took a whole new approach.

"In everything I did, I took baby steps. I felt the first time around I hadn't played it too smart—I was always the one who called Derek, always the one trying to make dinner plans, always the one hoping to get together. This time, I let him make more of an effort and didn't push things. I wasn't letting myself be totally exposed like I was last time. After graduation, he moved to New York for work, and I stayed in Philadelphia. The first few months, we only saw each other every other weekend. But finally things were going so well between us that there was no reason to hold back anymore. We've been dating steadily for two years now, and in fact, we just got engaged."

Yes, some couples do actually get back together—and sometimes, as Ashley and Derek can attest, it actually works. But with other couples, things don't pan out so well. Even if you and your ex both agree to get back into your relationship, it doesn't mean everything is automatically wonderful again. Sometimes, you're better off moving on than sticking it out.

That's a lesson that Brenda, age 27, learned the hard way. "Eddie and I first met on a blind date. We had a lot of chemistry, but he didn't want to get too involved, so he broke up with me after the first year. He said he felt he wasn't giving enough to me." But a month later, he asked to get back together, and she agreed.

Two years later, however, Eddie started making plans to move to Colorado. "He asked me to go with him, but I said no. I felt he was only asking because he was scared about the move and wanted someone to be there to ease his insecurity. I wasn't ready." Brenda wanted to pursue a long-distance relationship instead, but Eddie refused. "He said he didn't think it would work, so I was left brokenhearted again.

"Then about two months later, he started calling me and telling me how confused he was, how wrong he was, and how he wanted to come out and see me—and all of a sudden we were back in a relationship again." In the spring, Brenda

What If You Want Him Back?

went to visit Eddie in Colorado to discuss pre-engagement plans. "As soon as I got out there, something seemed wrong. After two days, he told me that if I moved out there, I needed to get my own place. He said he felt like he had changed. How could he have changed that much? I talked to him every single day. I found out later there was someone else he wanted to date, but he never told me that. I was so upset, I packed my bags and left, thinking, 'I can't do this anymore. He's never going to be happy.'

"Six months later, he called me late one night and said, 'I still care about you, and I know I hurt you.' I hung up. He called back and said, 'Please hear me out,' and told me again how much he cared about me. Then he started calling more and more—and the next thing I knew, we were seeing each other again!

"We visited each other a few times, but when I called him, he would act like he didn't have time for me. Although I didn't know it then, he had met someone else. After a few months, he said he didn't think it was a good idea for us to continue our relationship, and he broke up with me for the fourth time.

"Six months later, he invited me to a party for his parents' wedding anniversary. I loved his parents, and part of me wanted to see him, so I went. I made an effort to look like I was enjoying myself, but I was on the verge of tears the whole time. At one point, I saw a few pictures lying on a table—photos of Eddie with some girl. It was unsettling, but since this girl wasn't there, I figured maybe he still had a torch for me.

"A few days later, I called him and said, 'Look, I saw those pictures—is that your girlfriend? Are you in love with her?' He said yes and went on about how they had so much in common, but he didn't love her in the same way he loved me. He asked me, 'Do you marry your soul mate or someone you have the same interests with?'

"The minute he said that, I thought, 'What a crock!' It was the same way he pulled me in every time. He didn't feel enough for me to marry me, but now he's saying we're soul mates so he can have a safety net. He actually said to me, 'If we both turn thirty-two and we're not married, let's marry each other.' I was like, 'No way!' He's controlling and selfish. That just made it clear to me: I couldn't continue to see someone and give one hundred and ten percent but get fifty percent back."

Sadly, however, she still isn't totally over him. "Lately I've been thinking, I never tried to get back together with him. I think I should go back to Colorado in a fury and win him back," she says. "But I don't have the patience for it anymore. I feel that our love spoke for itself, and if he couldn't see that, forget it."

Whether he's taken you up on your offer to try again or suggested it on his own, think hard before you decide to go for it. Rushing into a reconciliation is never smart.

Lana, age 23, wishes she had waited. Despite a disastrous post-breakup sexual encounter, she and her ex remained friends—and before long they were back to something more. "Three months after the breakup, Joshua came to visit me, and we went out to dinner and a movie—it definitely felt like a date. Then he came back to my apartment and we made out. We ended up having sex again, and it was implied that we were getting back together.

"So we started seeing each other for the second time, but he was still very distant in that sort of 'I'm here but I'm thinking about being somewhere else' way. There was not that spark or connection that said if he didn't see me, he would be unhappy. I was always trying to make him feel good so he'd really love me. I was overly nice, not letting any peeves of mine grow into fights, massaging his ego, and not getting anything in return. There was no looking out for me—it was just, 'How can I make him happy and not get angry and show him how perfect I am?' Meanwhile, he was doing tons of work preparing for medical school and studying for the entrance exams. He started questioning his future and going through a really difficult time, but he refused any help from me.

"He broke up with me again two and a half months later, claiming we'd gotten back together too soon, and he still needed more time. He said, 'I love you, you're my ideal woman, and I still want to be with you one day. But right now I'm dead inside, and I have nothing to give you. I don't love you the way I used to.' He was not ready to grow up and commit the time it takes to have a life and a girlfriend."

Making It Work This Time

As Brenda and Lana can attest, it hurts enough getting your heart broken once. But having it happen a second (or third or fourth...) time with the same guy is true torture. So it pays to make sure you know what you're doing before you jump back into your old relationship. You've got to work out what happened the first time (see chapter 5 for more details) before you can expect the path to true love to run any more smoothly the second time around. "There's a tendency to want to attribute whatever problems the two of you had to situational factors, like the fact that he was really stressed-out with work," says Dr. Mojas. "But people have certain patterns of coping that appear in any stress situation. If he's sick for a week, he's likely to respond the same way. So don't even consider getting back into the relationship unless there's some attempt to deal with the patterns that caused it. If nothing's changed, there will be a honeymoon period, but then things will go right back to where they started."

Both of you are probably lugging around a lot of emotional baggage right now. If you don't unpack, chances are that the two of you won't have a very good time. That's why you should make a serious effort to talk about your problems—and possible solutions.

One way to approach this is for each of you to make a list of what you'd like the other to change. True, some men may balk at this idea, but if yours does, simply reiterate that it could be a major aid in your relationship's recovery. Even if you feel a little silly (and you might), try it anyway. Writing things down instead of just listing them off the top of your head may seem excessive, but it can really help keep the discussion productive instead of heated. See, when you write things down, you have more time to think about how to say them.

First rule: Phrase each item constructively. In other words, instead of saying, "I hate the way you never take me anywhere," say "I would like us to go out for a nice dinner once a week"; instead of saying "I want you to quit acting like a slob every time you come over," say "I would like you to clean up after yourself when you're at my place." You should each start by writing down five items on your lists. Then take turns going over your requests one by one and discussing whether they are things you each can agree to change.

Then, if there are more things you feel you need to talk about, you should each add those items. If your ex has two more major issues he wants to discuss, but you don't, write down a couple of minor things instead. It's important that you each have an equal number of items on your lists so you can take turns instead of feeling like one of you is haranguing the other. Again, discuss your problems one at a time, and see if you can come to a mutually agreeable solution.

When he elaborates on his complaints, make a concerted effort to *listen*, without being defensive, to what he's saying about how he feels and what he'd like to be different, and ask him to do the same when it's your turn. Remember, these are not personal attacks; they're relationship savers. Voicing your concerns is the first step to improving your relationship.

But don't expect miracles. Some things can be negotiated; others can't. "Look for a pattern and an attempt to do something about it," says Dr.

Mojas. "Some people tend to be very self-absorbed; your stuff is always in the background somehow. Others get very angry. Women are always trying to change these things. If it's something about his facial hair or the clothes he wears, fine, but if it's something on the inside—a character flaw you can't live with—be honest with yourself. We think once we're married or we've moved, he'll be more settled, or he won't be nasty to old women and children anymore. We think, 'If I'm just nice enough, or this enough, or that enough, things will get better.' " Guess again. As Dr. Mojas puts it, "Too many women live on that river in Egypt, De Nile."

If there's a major point neither of you will budge on (like he wants the two of you to get married and have kids but you don't want a family, or you want him to spend weekends with you but he wants to use that time to get ahead at work), you'll probably have to split up for good. But if you can both agree to what the other person would like to see change, you'll be on you way to a healthier, happier relationship.

Lana and Joshua are doing just that. Two months after her second breakup with Joshua, they decided to try again—but this time, to do it right. "I want him to accept help from me when he's down and to give me a commitment that the relationship will turn into a permanent thing," Lana says. In return, she's promised to spend more time on her own and let him see female friends without getting jealous. Working these issues out isn't easy, but they're taking things slowly and really communicating instead of ignoring the problems between them.

What If You Want Him Back?

If you're having trouble changing even when you both want to, consider going to couples counseling. Says Traci, age 25: "Scott and I broke up after two and a half years because we had major communication problems. That, coupled with his fear of commitment, paralyzed us. So when we talked about getting back together a few months down the road, we agreed to try couples therapy. We knew our problems would not go away on their own and had fears that, although we wanted to be together, we were just too different.

"Before we went to couples therapy, Scott and I never fought. I'd get mad at him for something he did or said, but then wouldn't say anything to him about my feelings. I'd just act like everything was cool and keep my anger bottled up inside, waiting for him to magically figure out I was mad at him. Then I'd gripe to all my friends about whatever it was I was upset about. He'd do the same thing, acting like everything was peachy even if he was totally mad. Sure, we never fought—but that was the problem!

"Once we started counseling, we learned how to communicate. If either of us was angry, we would say so right then and there. Like, I'd tell him, 'What you just said really pissed me off,' and we'd discuss it rather than just hiding things like we used to. Instead of letting our problems fester, we dealt with things immediately, and our relationship blossomed.

"Therapy gave us a safe environment for us to discuss things. Every relationship has big issues, and one of ours was marriage. We were getting serious, and people expected us to at least be engaged. The first time around, we were having problems dealing with the concept ourselves, much less with each other. Now we talk about it and it's not so scary. It's not like we always wonder what the other is thinking—we *know* what the other is thinking. Our relationship has totally changed."

But don't pin all your hopes on your old relationship. Sometimes, no matter how hard you try, your romance with your ex just can't be resuscitated. After all, you probably broke up because you just weren't right for each other. And since it's almost impossible to meet your soul mate when you're with your so-so mate, your ex may actually have done you a big favor by setting you free.

4

Okay, You're Still Obsessing

It's a month after the breakup. You're lying on the couch on a Saturday night watching MTV, and the video for Whitney Houston's "I Will Always Love You" comes on. You: a) plug your ears and run screaming from the room, b) start bawling like he just dumped you all over again, or c) throw a hammer at the television.

Right now, any of these may seem like a reasonable reaction (though the third option could turn into a pricey habit). You flash back to the good times. How his hair smelled. How he used to whisper in your ear. How he walked seventeen blocks in the snow to buy you Sudafed that Sunday you were sick. Why, why, why did he have to leave you?

If you still find yourself losing sleep, wearing black, and sobbing every time you hear a slow song, congratulations, you're normal. Of course, that's little consolation when normal feels so miserable.

When It's Not Just Your Heart That Hurts

"I would curl up in a fetal position all the time," says Ivy, age 27. "That's how I fell asleep, woke up, watched TV.... I felt weighed down more than anything. It was like having the flu for three weeks—I didn't have the energy to lift my head up. What was the point?"

You may actually find yourself physically ill. When James and I broke up, it wasn't just my heart that suffered. For two months, my whole body hurt: I lost my appetite, suffered from an upset stomach, got headaches. Jacqueline, age 32, says she lost twenty pounds in the months following her breakup. "I just didn't eat," she remembers.

Perhaps you're having trouble sleeping. "I was having night terrors," says Brenda, age 27. "I'd sleepwalk and wake up banging on the windows, trying to get out of my apartment. I also had insomnia, which really took its toll on me: I had a new job where I was working ten or twelve hours a day plus weekends, so it was hard being tired all the time. I hate the idea that I couldn't sleep because of Eddie, but that's what it was."

You may even get so deep-down sad, you can't think straight. After my breakup with James, for example, I would close my eyes at night and picture myself climbing out of my sixth-story bedroom window. All I wanted was an escape from my pain. I didn't actually want to die, but I did long to get out of that bed and away from the grief. Around this time, I wrote: "If he would just come back to me, it's like my life would suddenly be 100% better. I am in a lot of pain. This is making me so lonely and sad that I just cry and cry and cry."

Thinking his return would make everything worthwhile again was obviously misguided. But when all you can think about is your ex, it's hard to feel otherwise. This chapter will tell you how to *stop* focusing on him so you can *start* focusing on you.

He's Not Worth Dying Over

"I thought of killing myself a few times," says Brenda, age 27. "I was in an incredible depression. On top of the rejection and the betrayal, I was still in love with him. The relationship just felt like something I couldn't live without."

Sometimes, suicide seems like the answer. Jenni, age 25, says she completely freaked out after being jilted by her first love. Three weeks after the breakup, she jumped out of a pal's car at a stoplight and ran into moving traffic, hoping to get hit. Luckily, her friends chased her down and rushed her to a hospital. There, a doctor prescribed psychiatric drugs and therapy to help alleviate her depression. For a month or two she did feel better, but she was still haunted by thoughts of her ex.

Then one night she took a peek at some old pictures and love poems and fell completely over the edge. She tried to hang herself from her shower rod, but it snapped before her circulation was cut off. She broke down and sobbed for hours, reflecting on how easily her life could have been lost. That night, she vowed to get help. And now, three years later, she has a successful career, a healthy relationship, and—most importantly—a life.

You're in so much pain right now, it's hard to imagine a time you'll ever feel good again. If you and your ex can't be together, why go on? Plus, you might like the idea of making him sorry he didn't appreciate you more when you were alive. Your death will make him realize how much you really did mean to him—and show him the extent of your devotion: You love him so much you would rather die than live without him. Then there's the added bonus of his spending the rest of his life with the guilt of knowing he was responsible for your death.

Only it doesn't really work that way. If you kill yourself, it will only confirm to your ex that he was right—you were not the kind of person he wanted to be in a relationship with. After all, if you let him control your destiny to the extent that he decides whether you live or die, your relationship could never be healthy.

"Finally, I realized that no one should make you feel that way," says Brenda, age 27. "It made me mad that he had that much power over me."

No matter how bad the breakup, suicide should never be an option. If you find yourself thinking about it a lot, planning out how you would do it, or even composing a suicide note in your head, seek help. Call the American Suicide Foundation at 1-800-ASF-4042 from 9 A.M. to 5 P.M. Eastern Time, Monday through Friday, for a referral to a suicide prevention hotline in your area. Or call Covenant House's 24-hour Nine

Line: 1-800-999-9999. You may also want to ask a couple of friends if it's okay to call them in the middle of the night if you start feeling like you might go through with it.

Keep these numbers with you at all times, and pick up the phone whenever you feel the need. You don't have to face this alone. In addition to these precautionary measures, get yourself into therapy immediately (see page 169 for guidelines on this) to help you deal with the deeper issues that are making you consider suicide.

Stop Blaming Yourself

"Pat was my first love," says Laura, age 25. "We met at the restaurant where we both worked, and the attraction between us was instant. After we'd dated about six months, we decided to move to Key West. Things were great at first—we ate fresh crab legs and talked about getting married and having water babies. But we lived with two other people, and that was hard. Pat and one of our roommates, Fiona, fought a lot, and Fiona's boyfriend was really into heavy drugs, which I didn't like. Plus, I desperately missed my friends and family back in Oklahoma. So, although Pat wanted to stay, we packed our bags after only four months.

"On the way home, we stopped in Memphis to visit Pat's parents. After we were there a few days, I found an application he'd filled out for a job at a restaurant near his parents' place. When I asked him what the deal was, he said he was going to stay with his parents for a while to make some money.

"I was devastated, but I thought we would continue our relationship long-distance. Once I got back to Oklahoma, however, he wouldn't return any of my calls. I wrote him a letter saying I wanted us to be together, but I couldn't just sit there and wait without his even trying. A few weeks later, I got a letter from him saying it was better for us to be apart. I completely lost it. All I could think about was Pat, Pat, Pat.

"A few months later, I found out from a mutual friend that Pat was back in Florida. Even though I never got the money together to do it, I wanted so badly to transfer to a school down there and 'accidentally' run into him. I was sure we'd see each other again and felt I had to look perfect. I worked out a lot and tanned; I even got a nose job with him in mind. I always planned our happenstance meeting—he'd be working in a bar, I'd go in, and he'd be blown away. I just thought, 'Damn, he won't believe how great I look now—I'm like a different person. Not like the person who moved away from Florida and caused the breakup.'

"I now realize I should have been more adult and laid-back about everything and not gotten so homesick. I just wish I hadn't gotten in the middle of Pat and Fiona's fights or let things like Fiona's boyfriend doing drugs bother me as much as they did. At nineteen, I'd never been exposed to that before, but now that wouldn't faze me at all—I'd just go with the flow more. To this day, I think if I could've stuck it out in Florida, we would still be together. I still can't stop kicking myself for the mistakes I made six years ago."

Clearly, Laura isn't being fair to herself. "You can't torture yourself by going over and over what happened, wondering if there was one thing you could have done differently," says Dr. Mojas. "Women are much more likely than men to think it's something they did. Men think, 'Well, she just wasn't right for me.'" When wallowing in your woe becomes your usual way of approaching the world, it's not a good thing. Self-blame, however, isn't the answer.

Certainly, you should accept responsibility for any part you may have played in the breakdown of your relationship. (To learn more about this, see chapter 5.) But that doesn't mean you should excuse your ex's behavior. Perhaps he ignored you, criticized you, or severely cut down the amount of time you spent together toward the end of your relationship—and then blamed you for his behavior. Maybe he even told you he had no choice but to break up with you because you were pressuring him for a commitment, or you didn't trust him enough, or you were too demanding.

You may start to wonder if he's right. Maybe if you were just less pushy, acted less jealous, or stopped nagging so much, you'd be together. But what you don't realize is that you were probably reacting to his pulling away. Once your ex started to withdraw, it almost didn't matter what you did. By the time the two of you finally broke up, your ex was probably just looking for an excuse to say sayonara.

It could even be something trivial, seemingly random. "Luke and I had been living together for two years, and one night I broached the subject of marriage," Melissa, age 33, recalls. "Actually, we had discussed it before, but never this seriously. But this time Luke told me he didn't want to get married. He liked things the way they were and had no intention of tying the knot. He said he loved me, but that we didn't have similar enough interests—most importantly, I didn't own Rollerblades!"

However serious or silly his reasons, you may wish for another chance to prove yourself. Since you broke the relationship, you can fix it, right? Now that you realize what you were doing wrong, you'll stop, and everything will be okay again. This time you'll try harder, never mention the M word again, buy a pair of Rollerblades! But he's already tried. For whatever reason, which may well have more to do with him than you, he's already given up on the relationship. If you're the only one trying now, there's no way it will work. Self-blame is self-defeating. It takes two to build a relationship, and it takes two to maintain one. If he's given up, that's his fault, not yours.

Ultimately, you've got to realize that you can't be responsible for anyone's decisions but your own. "You may keep asking yourself, 'Why doesn't he want me?'" says Dr. Peterson. "But he may have his own individual issues. For instance, he may have a fear of intimacy. Men are socialized not to open up; to be intimate means having to be vulnerable. Or he may have had bad experiences with other women—experiences that have nothing to do with you. Unfortunately, sometimes it's easier for a guy to say 'This isn't working' rather than to deal with his emotional issues.

"Suppose you really would be great for him. There's a tendency to think 'I've got to make him see it!' But you can't make him see anything. He may not see it for ten years, not until after you're happily married to someone else. Your relationship won't work unless he wants it to. You could have Cindy Crawford's body, Einstein's mind, and Jay Leno's sense of humor, but it wouldn't matter if he's not ready. It hurts, but you've got to accept it and move on."

Obsess on Purpose

It's easy to focus on the good memories now and let the bad ones fade into the background. That's human nature, especially if he was the one who rejected you. "But if you find that you're spending a good deal of your time thinking, 'I wonder what he's doing right now,' or remembering his cute little dimple, it could be a problem," warns Hillyer. "Of course you're going to think about him a lot in the beginning, but if you can't concentrate on your work or your friends or anything else, and it's not easing off within a few months, ask yourself, 'Am I getting off on my drama?'

"If the answer is yes, do you want to stay with it? You may find that really getting into your drama works as a healing process. Put on some melancholy music, get out all his pictures, and go for it. Sometimes an evening of that will make you sick and tired of obsessing and help you get on with your life."

You could even plan an obsession time every day. Set aside anywhere from ten minutes to an hour a day to focus just on him. The rest of the time, don't let yourself think about your old relationship at all. If you start to daydream about your ex, stop and set those thoughts aside until it's time. That's when you can reflect and cry all you want. This will help you remain calm while at work, standing in line at the post office, or choosing cantaloupes at the grocery store.

Making your obsession time as uninviting as possible will encourage you to cut down the amount of time you devote to it. Plan to obsess while the news is on if you usually look forward to watching it every night. Make yourself uncomfortable. Sit in a hard-back chair; take it outside if the weather's unpleasantly hot or cold. Afterward, do something fun to congratulate yourself for all the time you didn't spend obsessing that day and to reinforce the idea that you could be enjoying life instead of wasting your time thinking about him.

You may soon tire of your obsession sessions and be tempted to go back to obsessing on and off again throughout the day. But give it a chance. If you find it tedious, that's good. Gradually cut down the amount of time you're devoting to it until you no longer feel the need to obsess at all.

Dealing with Betrayal

"I was living in Philadelphia, but Matt was going to school in New York," says Ann, age 28. "I went to visit him one weekend and planned to meet him in his dorm, so he left me the key to his room. But when I got up there, I saw a copy of a note that he had sent me with flowers—only this one had another girl's name on it. He had sent the same note to some girl named Donna! I didn't know what to do. There were no more trains out that night, so I was stuck there. He came back to the room all happy, and I just said, 'I hope Donna liked the flowers!'

"That should have been the end of the relationship, but it was just the beginning of the end. We said we'd stop seeing each other, but he came down to Philly for a wedding, and we ended up sleeping together. He called a few weeks later and said he wanted to come visit. I said he could come only if we could spend some quality time together. He agreed and arrived at one in the morning. We went to bed. When he woke up, he said he had to go back to New York for a party. That night, he called me at three A.M. to tell me he'd asked Donna to stop by, and did I think she would be mad if he wasn't at home? That was it. We didn't speak for two years after that."

If he cheated on you, your feelings of abandonment and rejection may seem overwhelming. You wonder why you weren't good enough for him, but that's not what made him stray: He probably cheated because he felt horny, insecure, trapped, or angry at you. No matter how bruised your self-esteem is, you have to realize that infidelity is an inappropriate response to any of these emotions. Clearly, he wasn't putting the value on your relationship that it deserved. Otherwise he wouldn't have let his lust get the best of him, and he would have talked to you about whatever difficulties the two of you were having rather than thinking he'd solve them by hopping into bed with someone else. "If he's been unfaithful, remember that it's not about you," says Dr. Cooper. "It's his problem. Yes, there may have been problems in the relationship, but if he wanted to go out with other people, he should have had the balls to tell you that."

So don't let his current behavior stir up your sense of competition and rivalry. Forget about checking up on him or stalking him. You are no longer dating, remember? And it's a good thing, because he obviously doesn't deserve your trust or love.

Or maybe he started seeing someone seriously just six days after he left you. Maybe you've even heard he's getting married. It doesn't matter if he was fooling around behind your back or not—you still feel hurt and betrayed. How could he move on so quickly? But instead of getting jealous or down on yourself, be glad you got away from him. The fact that he's rushing into another relationship is an indication of his immaturity. Getting involved with someone new may be his way of dealing with his guilt over ending your relationship. But chances are, his inability to cope with difficult emotions will come back to haunt him. Luckily, this time you won't be the one who has to contend with the consequences.

Whether or not your jealousy and anger are warranted, they can still keep you living in the past. That's what happened to Lana, age 23. "What led to the breakup was a visit from a female friend Joshua had met while overseas for a semester. I knew she was interested in him because I'd found a letter she'd sent him saying, 'I hope I didn't make you feel uncomfortable when I told you my feelings about you.' Anyway, she was going to visit him for a month, starting at the end of December. I wasn't pleased. I mean, he barely had time for me, yet he could spend a month entertaining this girl. I was also upset because I wasn't looking forward to spending New Year's Eve with my boyfriend and his secret admirer. So I ended up being cold to her on New Year's, and when we got home Joshua broke up with me. He said he couldn't be in a relationship with someone who couldn't get along with his friends."

Since Lana and Joshua went to the same college, she dreaded going back the next semester. "I wanted to drop out of school. I was very depressed. I was constantly thinking about him having a great time with this other girl. But once I went back to college, I felt better. Classes were going well, and I made new friends and started going out more."

If you let the old relationship control your life, you may do things you'll later regret. Lana could have let her jealousy and feelings of rejection convince her to quit school. But what good would that have done her? What he does now—and who he's doing it with—shouldn't concern you or make you feel inadequate.

Oh, Sweet Revenge

He broke up with you, and now he's going to pay. You'll break into his apartment and steal his

Best of Jenny McCarthy video collection. Or have twenty Domino's pizzas sent over to his house every other Monday at midnight. Or even call the phone company and have his number disconnected. Whatever you do to him, you're certain it won't be anywhere near as bad as what he put you through.

While researching this chapter, I encountered quite a few women whose day of reckoning could have earned them several days in jail. While I in no way suggest that you try anything even remotely resembling these out-of-control, *Fatal Attraction*-ish tactics, there may be some comfort in knowing that while your revenge fantasies might be outlandish, at least they (hopefully) aren't as crazy as some that other women have actually acted on. . . .

- slashing the tires on his car
- smashing his windshield
- keying and spray painting his car
- calling his boss and saying bad things about him
- throwing potted plants through his windows
- pouring urine into his gas tank
- giving his calling-card number to friends around the globe

Okay, so these take-no-prisoners tactics aren't real mature. But considering how much pain he's caused you, it's only natural to want to cause him pain right back. Of course, it's crossed your mind, but you wouldn't actually do anything. Or would you?

Revenge Between the Sheets

"Jim cheated on me and then dumped me," says Mavis, age 20. "Well, he hurt me, so I hurt him: I slept with his best friend's brother, who was like a brother to him.

"I didn't speak to Jim for a long time. But then I contacted him on his birthday and was all nice, pretending I still liked him, and invited him to spend the night at my parents' lake house.

"I slept with him that night and then never called him again. I went back to college, never said good-bye, and refused to return his calls. I wanted him to see how it felt to feel used and to be taken advantage of. I treated him badly so he'd feel just as terrible as I did when we broke up. Well, I got my malicious streak out, and we called it even."

Think sleeping with your ex's best friend is extreme? Not when you're dealing with avenging a broken heart, apparently: One woman I met claimed she slept with her ex's *dad* after the breakup. (Kids, don't try this at home!)

In fact, don't try any of this, period. According to Dr. Mojas, "Realistically, you will have thoughts of revenge, but if you're acting on them, do not pass go, do not collect two hundred dollars—get yourself to a therapist immediately. You're out of control with your destructive behavior, and you need help with that. You're dealing with a rage that's not just about the end of a relationship."

Dr. Peterson agrees. "Revenge is a waste of energy that could be used for healing. It also leaves no room for anyone else to get into your heart. Instead of spending your time finding a new love, you'd rather spend it getting back at someone. It's a cruel and empty victory."

Vindictive Visualization

Of course, just because revenge is unhealthy doesn't mean you can't spend a little time thinking about it. Fantasizing about revenge on your ex reminds you that you're no longer a victim. Think about all the things you could do to make his life hell: Write to the IRS and report the taxes he didn't pay; call his fundamentalist mother and tell her he's not a virgin; let his boss know he was the one who was stealing all the staples. Feels good to know you could ruin his life whenever you felt like it, doesn't it?

And, best of all, you can think up revenge schemes driving to work in the morning, sitting at your desk during the day, even while you're out at night with someone new. That's what Dawn, age 30, did: "I had been seeing this guy I worked with, Robert, and it was a really messy breakup. Well, a few months later, a new guy started working in my office. We were friends at first, but then he asked me out, and that night, he ended up coming back to my place and staying over. Since it was during the week, we had go to work the next day and I had to give him something to wear so he wouldn't show up at the office in the exact same outfit twice in a row.

"I was very tempted to give the new guy one of the shirts that Robert had left behind at my apartment. He and Robert sit really close to each other at the office, and they were very distinctive T-shirts—it would have been immediately apparent where it came from. But in the end, I decided it wasn't worth it. I didn't want it to get out that I was involved with the new guy, and besides, I didn't want to give Robert the satisfaction of knowing that I was still thinking about him."

Good move. Sure, it's fun to daydream about punishing him for the way he treated you, but keep in mind that actually acting on it would ultimately just set you back. Besides, getting revenge is only inviting retaliation from your ex, and you don't need to get hurt even more right now. Just thinking about the pain you could inflict on him and talking about it with friends can be just as satisfying (and a lot less dangerous) than breaking into his apartment and filling his tub with piranhas.

The Power of the Poisonous Pen

You may even want to do a little therapeutic creative writing and pen a short story or two starring you as the charming, beautiful heroine and your ex as the evil villain or the loser everyone hates. After all, who knows what could come of writing it all down? Just ask Julie, age 25. Although her ex pulled one lame move after another, in the end, she got the last word.

"Jason and I both worked together in the same restaurant. We started dating, and after about six months, moved in with each other. Shortly thereafter, we bought this puppy together, which

I thought symbolized a lot. It felt like having a kid in a weird way, since we both had to commit to it. Well, one night I was in bed and Jason was wasted—at this point, he was drinking about twelve beers a day. As it turned out, he was lying on the living-room floor throwing the puppy all the way up to the ceiling and then catching it. Then all of a sudden I hear the dog yelping—of course, he missed.

"We took the dog to the vet, and it turned out to have a broken leg and hip. It was twelve hundred dollars for the surgery. Of course, I paid for it; Jason didn't have any money. At one point, he actually pawned my VCR because he was so broke. Still I stayed with him. But the dog episode was the beginning of the end.

"The actual breakup took place after his ex called one night when we were supposed to be going out to dinner. I was just waiting for him to get off the phone, and they talked for an hour and a half, so I was pissed. The next day, Jason said I couldn't handle him being friends with his ex and then went on to tell me he didn't want to marry me anyway, so why continue the relationship? I told him I didn't want to marry him, either. It was over.

"I wanted to end things on good terms, so when he moved into his new apartment, I paid for his deposit and some of his moving expenses. Then he told me I owed him three hundred dollars for the dog, since we'd bought it together and I was taking it, and I actually gave him the money. As if that weren't enough, a couple of months after he moved out, his electricity got cut off because he hadn't paid his bill, and he asked

Okay, You're Still Obsessing

me if he could stay with me for the weekend, until he could get it turned on again.

"That weekend turned into seven weeks. Every time he got money, he just spent it. He kept saying he was waiting for his student loan check to come in, and he'd give me five hundred dollars for letting me stay with him, but nothing ever came of it. In fact, I saw him once at a club several months later and the first thing he said to me was, 'You're never going to see the money I owe you.'

"The thing that makes me sickest is that I let him get away with everything for so long. When we were living together, he would have parties and blast music late at night, so I had to put a sleeping bag in our walk-in closet in order to sleep when he had people over. I adored him so much—he was my first love and was so sweet to me in the beginning. But those good times sure didn't make up for the fact he was such a jerk to me in the end.

"My dad finally gave me the strength to kick Jason out. I was bitching about him one night, and Dad said, 'Julie, I love you, but the guy doesn't have a gun to your head. If you're going to let him do this to you, don't complain about it.' That night I went home and told Jason he'd have to be out that weekend. He said he understood. I packed all his stuff for him and even wrote him a note wishing him good luck, but when I got home from work on Sunday night, he was asleep on my couch. When I told him he had to leave, he was like, 'My check's coming this week. . . . ' I told him he still had to go. So he called me a selfish bitch and threw my apartment key in my face. I was crying and felt like a total doormat. It was almost like we were breaking up once more."

However, in the end, she gave him his just desserts by putting her story to paper. "Basically, he didn't respect me in any sense of the word, and I vowed to make him sorry. While I was dating him, I took this creative writing class and started a story with a character loosely based on him. After we broke up, I began working on it a lot, and the story turned into a novel. All my anger at him came through in the book. In fact, I had a little sign with the quote YOU ARE NOTHING—something Jason actually said to me during one of our fights—over my computer. When I wanted to quit writing, I would look at that quote and it would spur me on.

"Once I finished the book, wanting to get it published became less about him and more about advancing my career and making my family proud and doing something positive for me. But if I hadn't wanted to prove to Jason that I was something, if I hadn't spent all that time imagining him seeing my book in a bookstore, I might never have gotten it done. Now it's getting published, and thousands can read about the evil that is my ex-boyfriend! Actually, I no longer hate Jason. After all, if I hadn't gone through that awful breakup, I might not be a published novelist."

Unexpected Revenge

Imagine yourself walking down the street with the perfect guy—you know, the one with the great teeth who writes you long love letters even

Okay, You're Still Obsessing

though he lives next door—and running into your ex, who drools all over you, begging you to take him back. Now imagine yourself saying, "Too late, Romeo!", laughing in his face and walking off with Mr. Close-Up. Feels good, doesn't it?

Hey, could happen. "You usually get revenge when you least expect it," says Amelia, age 27. "When my first boyfriend broke up with me, it really hurt. I was still in love with him and long hoped we'd get back together, but when my fantasy became a reality, I didn't take him up on it: Eight years later, he told me he was finally ready for a commitment—but at that point, I was seeing someone else. He'd counted on my being there for eight years, so when I rejected *him*, he found it really painful."

Twenty-four-year-old Abby had a similar experience. "I had been dating Nicholas for two years when he moved to another state. Trying to continue our relationship was difficult for me; I think it's always harder for the one being left than for the one leaving. I missed him immensely and was just head over heels for him.

"My birthday fell on Thanksgiving that year, and he had planned to fly in and spend the day with me. I was so excited—I had just lost five pounds, it was my birthday, and my boyfriend was coming to visit. He was supposed to pick me up at home at eleven-thirty in the morning . . . but he never showed. I sat at my kitchen table until seven-thirty P.M. and didn't move; I guess I was in shock. When I finally got ahold of him at his parents' house at ten o'clock that night, he told me he just didn't love me anymore. I was devastated."

But Nicholas lived to regret it. "I bumped into him the next year while we were both back home visiting our parents. It was every girl's dream situation. I looked and felt really good, and he was saying things like, 'I'm so sorry. You're so great. I can't believe I let you go. I want you back—please take me back.' I just looked him in the eye and said, 'Sorry, buddy—you lost your chance!' By that time, I was living in a different city, had all these new friends, and was seeing a few different guys. After everything Nicholas had done to me, it felt wonderful turning him down."

Positive Paybacks

You may also find satisfaction in enjoying all the stuff he didn't want you doing while you were dating. Stay out all night long. Eat ice cream for breakfast. Play strip poker at your next party. Wear that really low-cut red dress he said made you look cheap but you think you look great in. Daydream about what his reaction would be if he caught you doing these things, and then picture your retort: "I don't care what you think anymore. It's my life, and I'll live it as I see fit."

Finally, think up some positive ways to punish him. Maybe he'll be the reason you go after that promotion you've been dreaming about. Maybe now you'll be motivated to go to step class at your gym every morning. Or maybe you'll finally find the time to expand your mind by visiting museums on Sunday afternoons. Self-improvement nearly always makes you feel better—and him feel worse for letting you go. Yes, it's true: Living well really is the best revenge. And if you're happy, you'll eventually stop caring about making him sorry.

"I still think about getting revenge on him for the way he treated me. I do. But that will pass. He's not worth it," says Debbie, age 28. "My revenge has been that I've gone on with my life. I have surprised myself. I am much more at ease on my own than when I was with him. Because his problems will remain unaddressed, he'll get his in the end—that's how it works."

Get Mad, Not Even

To help you reframe your relationship in a more realistic, less rosy light, take note of your ex's faults and transgressions. Here's how.

1. Write down every trait he had that you disliked: He was consistently rude to waiters and salespeople; too serious to get half your jokes; so cheap he wouldn't go out to dinner unless he had a coupon for the restaurant.
2. Add everything he ever did that made you angry: He stood you up for your best friend's wedding, opting to go to a hockey game with the guys; bought you a kielbasa for Christmas, claiming he forgot you were a vegetarian; refused to answer the call-waiting beep, even though he was using *your* phone and you were

expecting a long-distance call from your ailing grandma.

3. List all the things he tried to get you to do that bugged the hell out of you: He forced you to accompany him to Jean-Claude van Damme movies; dragged you deep-sea fishing; woke you up in the middle of the night to have sex every time he had a dream about Pamela Anderson Lee.

4. Next, make a note of what you needed that you weren't getting from your ex. What great characteristics do you have that he didn't like or never even seemed to notice? What do you want from your next relationship that your old one didn't provide?

5. Then get your friends to help: Ask them what they really thought of your ex. At first, they may be hesitant; they know you loved him and think they'll upset you if they say anything negative. They may also be concerned that you and your ex will get back together, so any criticisms they share with you will come back to haunt them. Simply assure them that you won't hold anything they say against them, and in fact, you need them to help you get through your grieving process. Ask them for assistance when you're already a little mad about your ex's insensitivity and general boorishness; that way, you're less likely to turn defensive.

If you fear that having your friends reel off your ex's bad qualities will make you feel like a fool for going out with him in the first place, you need to remember that you, like everyone else, make mistakes sometimes. Sure, you could close your eyes to your ex's faults and pretend the whole thing never happened, but unless you acknowledge his bad points, you'll never learn from your negative experiences.

Share a few of the items on your list to get your pals started. Until now, you may have kept certain things from them because you were embarrassed about dating someone who acted that way. Likewise, they've probably kept things from you. You may even find out he lied to you or made a pass at your best friend. No matter what you're hearing now, focus on feeling angry, not hurt. Remember, the jerk is out of your life. Good riddance!

Each time you start to get nostalgic for your old, "perfect" relationship, take out the list for an instant reality check. It's proof that your relationship wasn't as wonderful as you remember. And each time you start to feel that you're the reason it didn't work, consult your list: Here's evidence of the many ways your *ex* dropped the ball.

Carry your list with you. That way, whenever you think of something else to add, you can jot it down. Turning your pain into anger is an important step in getting past your loss. Instead of feeling sorry that he isn't with you anymore, start feeling exasperated, annoyed, furious. It's too bad he was too short-sighted to try again with you. You know how much you cared for him, despite all the bad stuff. Do you really want to be with a guy who can't even recognize how great he had it?

Twelve More Ways to Get Him Out of Your Head

1. *Visualize yourself literally closing the door on your old relationship.* Imagine putting your ex and all your old feelings about him in a dark room and then shutting the door. As you walk away from the room, picture the hall in front of you filling with light.
2. *Practice a psychological technique called thought-stopping.* You will feel ridiculous doing this, but try it anyway—it really works! At a time when you're feeling calm and in control, make a list of the obsessive thoughts you've been having. One example: "How could he leave me when our love was so good?" Say it out loud, but when you get to the word *good*, clap your hands as hard as you can and yell "Stop!" Recite your sentence again, but this time, clap and yell "Stop!" on the second-to-last word. Repeat, leaving off one more word each time, until eventually you clap and yell "Stop!" after the first word.

   Keep practicing until you can hear the clapping and the "Stop!" in your mind instead of having to hear them out loud. That way, when you start to have that recurring thought, you'll automatically stop yourself. You gain control over your obsessing and take responsibility for interrupting the thoughts that cause you the most distress. If you like, you can even wear a rubber band around your wrist and snap it every time you start to think about him; that will reinforce the clapping and the "Stop!" in your head.

If you're having trouble, remember that it's *your* mind, and you're in control. Judy Kuriansky, Ph.D. (better known as Dr. Judy), a clinical psychologist in private practice in New York City and cohost of the nationally syndicated radio show *LovePhones*, suggests this exercise in her book *The Complete Idiot's Guide to Dating* (Alpha Books, 1996): "Think about your ex. Now think about being in love with someone else. Now think about your ex. Now think about getting a raise at work. Now think about laughing with a new friend. Now think about a pink elephant. See how you can control your thoughts?"

3. *Buy a plastic bat at a toy store and use it.* "Take the bat to a pillow and let your feelings out," says Joan Childs. "It's a great way to discharge the anger, disappointment, and hurt. This will help you exorcise him from your mind."

4. *Stop questioning your entire relationship and personal worth.* Did he ever truly care about you? It's easy to doubt his feelings for you, especially if your breakup was messy. Maybe he even said he never loved you. Maybe he ripped your picture in half or told you he hated your guts.

But there must have been something about you that attracted him in the first place. Think of your friends and family and all the other people who reassure you that you're special—you know you're a good person with many wonderful qualities. Chances are, he felt more for you than he's admitting now; he may only be telling himself he never really cared in order to justify ending your relationship. Or maybe he's too messed up to truly love anyone. Whatever his personal issues, the important thing to realize is that you are worth loving—and that you can find someone who will appreciate you.

5. *Keep a record of what you're going through.* Sometimes just getting your thoughts out of your head and down on paper can help you work through your emotions. As Virginia, age 26, explains, "Charles and I went to school together, so even after we broke up, I continued to see him quite often. When he'd do something to totally upset me, I'd write about it in my journal. It enabled me to get my feelings out—especially since he refused to speak to me—and explore them on my own."

You may even want to make a rule for yourself that each time you start thinking about him, you'll write down your thoughts in your journal. Having to carry it with you, take it out, and jot down your feelings every single time he comes to mind will discourage you from spending too much time obsessing over him.

6. *Lean on your friends.* When they ask you if there's anything they can do, tell them. Take advantage of their offers: If you're going through a rough time and you want them to stay with you for a few days, ask. If you'd like them to just go out for ice cream with you, say so.

Have long phone conversations with old friends and family members. Call them on the spur of the moment if you're really down; let them comfort you. Talking to them will also give you the opportunity to catch up on all the loved ones in your life besides your ex.

But don't ask your friends for information about him. If he's doing well, you'll feel sad. (Doesn't he miss me? Isn't he suffering, too?) If he seems upset, it could give you false hope. (Will he come back? Should I call him to commiserate?) Besides, he's bound to hear through the grapevine that you're asking about him, which doesn't do much for your dignity. Avoid this altogether by asking your friends not to tell you if they've seen him or heard about him lately.

Acknowledge friends who are especially supportive by doing something nice for them. Say thanks by baking them cookies, sending them a small bouquet of flowers, or taking them out to dinner. They deserve it!

7. *Watch movies and reread books that you loved and your ex hated*, to help you remember how different you were. How could you have been in a relationship with someone who fell asleep during *The English Patient*? How could you have dated someone—seriously, no less—who couldn't get through more than ten pages of *The Fountainhead*?

8. *Surround yourself with living things*. Get a pet if you've always wanted one. Or buy a plant or two. Knowing that something needs you

and watching it grow can help you feel better. Since my breakup, I've felt a small sense of reward with every new leaf on my hanging ivy and every new sprout on my philodendron. As silly as it sounds, they depend on me, and I'm taking good care of them.

9. *Exercise.* According to Dr. Cooper, it builds up serotonin in the brain, which is just what Prozac does. Although going for a run or heading to an aerobics class may sound like a pain, working out will actually make you happier and healthier, plus help you deal with your depression. Not to mention the fact that you'll look and feel great!

10. *Break the sex connection.* Instead of fantasizing about your ex, imagine being in bed with Brad Pitt. If your mind always seems to drift back to your ex, use thought-stopping to help you refocus on Brad. But don't try to replace your ex by sleeping with someone else right away. You may think bedding a good friend or new acquaintance is just what you need, but in fact, it's only likely to create a whole new set of problems. (See pages 220 and 230 for more guidelines on getting back into the sexual swing of things.)

    Instead, do other sensual things for yourself. Get a massage. Take a swim in the ocean. Give your best friend a hug. Eat expensive chocolates. Buy a vibrator! Indulge yourself, and you won't feel so bad about being alone.

11. *Put things in perspective.* "Balance comes to mind," says Dr. Lutwin. "It's not your entire life. It's an event—a relationship. You should

try to process and understand it rather than get stuck obsessing about it." If you're having a great deal of difficulty doing this, consider therapy. (See page 169 for more details.)

12. *Give up hope for the relationship*, even if you don't want to disconnect from him. "I didn't want to let go of the pain," says Brenda, age 27. "I wanted to feel like he was still a part of my life, even if it hurt." Sometimes, we invest so much into a relationship that we don't want to let it end. Even if you never see him, in your mind you're still half of that happy couple. When you feel you can't go on without him, there seems to be no choice but to hang on to the heartache.

    But what if you allowed yourself to let the hurt go? You'd have to start over, work on a whole new self-concept. Yes, this is scary. But delaying it doesn't make it any easier. The sooner you accept your loss, the sooner you can heal.

    In order to get over him, you have to decide the relationship is beyond saving, just as he's already done. Stop wishing he'd change, making up schemes to get him back, fantasizing about a reunion, and planning how you'll make him happier next time. Until you believe it's over, you'll be stranded. So tell your family, your friends, and yourself that you're through. And don't make yourself available to him. Instead of investing hope in your past, invest hope in your future. Make a commitment to yourself and your healing.

Once you've kicked him out of your heart and head and established your own identity again, you'll be able to see both the bad and the good in the relationship. Eventually, you'll get to the point where you can look at it honestly and clearly, be able to forgive yourself and your ex, and move on with your life. There will be ups and downs—you can't expect complete healing all at once—but you do have a future beyond your ex.

Twenty Things You Could Be Doing Instead of Thinking About Him

1. Get a manicure
2. Go for a long walk, bike ride, or drive (no, not past his house)
3. Try a new recipe
4. Take a belly-dancing class
5. Watch old home movies with your family
6. Buy a new perfume
7. Take a sketchbook to the park and try your hand at landscape drawing
8. Visit your favorite museum
9. Cook dinner for your parents
10. Read a new mystery novel
11. Gather all your friends and have a snowball fight
12. Plant a garden
13. Paint your nails
14. Fantasize about someone new
15. Sew a new dress

Okay, You're Still Obsessing

16. Invite a friend you've lost touch with to go out for coffee with you
17. Clean out your closet and give old clothes to charity
18. Take an extra-long hot shower
19. Go dancing with the girls
20. Make yourself an ice-cream sundae, complete with hot fudge, whipped cream, jimmies, and a cherry on top

5

What Went Wrong

If you thought that patterns were just for dressmaking, guess again. We all have certain behavioral patterns that appear over and over in our relationships. To find out what yours are, you can start by looking at your relationship with your ex. If you can figure out why it crashed and burned, you may be able to learn how to prevent your next relationship from meeting the same fate—and discover a lot about yourself in the process. As Dr. Mojas puts it, "Instead of getting depressed or getting even, the way to get over him is to get curious."

After all, your breakup can teach you a lot. "You feel you lose a part of yourself if you walk away because you invested so much in the relationship," Mojas continues. "But the reality is that you also gain something: You've learned what you don't want from a relationship, and you've also learned something about what you do want. And just because you can't get it from your ex doesn't mean you can't have it. Maybe the reason you were with this man in the first place was to clarify what you want from your next relationship—and that's a gift you get to keep."

Get Another Opinion

Enlisting the help of a third party can help you see the dynamics of your relationship more clearly. Have you ever noticed that one of your friends consistently gets into certain kinds of relationships and falls into certain types of behavior, yet seems completely unaware of what she's doing? Here's a shocker: She might be thinking the exact same thing about you.

"Ask your friends, 'What did I complain about the most?' and 'What did you not want to tell me about the relationship then that you can tell me now?'" suggests Dr. Mojas. "They may say something like, 'Well, I noticed that every time we went out, he ordered for you, and when you said, "Hey, I don't like fish," he'd say, "Well, just try it." Or maybe you were anxious, censored yourself, acted more passive, lost your sense of humor.... Maybe you always seemed really critical of him or constantly complained. Your friends can help you identify your pattern of tolerating intolerable behavior or denying a blind spot about your own actions."

But don't stop there. You should also ask, "'When I was with him, was I myself? The way I am with you?'" Dr. Peterson advises. "Often, the answer will be no. But if you can't be your real self around a guy, then he's not for you. And that might be why it didn't work."

If there's no one to help you figure out what happened because no one you're close to really got to know him, that tells you something too: You knew there was something wrong, and it wasn't safe to bring the relationship out into the world. Why would you get involved with someone you didn't want other people you care about to get to know? As you consider this question, don't bother thinking up excuses for your past; instead, focus on making changes for your future.

Accept Your Contribution to the Breakup

In order to learn from your experience, you have to accept some responsibility for what happened. Whether you feel guilty about your own behavior or regret that you tolerated his, figuring out where you messed up is crucial; otherwise you won't know what to do differently the next time you fall in love.

It's possible that you made it difficult for your ex to stay in the relationship. Think back. Consult your journal. What did he complain about the most? Were you too controlling? Did you nag and criticize too much? Were you so focused on your career that you didn't give him enough time and attention? Maybe you were so anxious to marry him that you became dependent and clingy. Or perhaps you're afraid of commitment, so you kept him at a permanent distance. Whatever the problem was, ask yourself if the same thing has happened with other boyfriends in the past. If so, it points to a pattern that you need to be aware of.

On the other hand, maybe you feel he did you wrong. But you have to dig deeper than "he's a jerk" to learn anything. After all, you got into a relationship with him. Why?

To find out, suggests Dr. Peterson, "play back the video of your life with him. Wasn't there a sign fairly early on that something was wrong? Didn't your intuition tell you, maybe even the first day, that something wasn't up to par? But you chose to ignore it because he was cute or you were lonely. If we ignore that intuition, we usually find out later that we were right."

Jacqueline, age 32, discovered that firsthand. "The first night Andrew and I went out, I came home and told my roommates, 'I have to stay away from this man!' He'd said he was in the middle of a messy breakup, but I think he was actually cheating on someone with me. I had a gut feeling that this guy was bad news, but I ignored it. I was twenty-three and more interested in having a tumultous relationship, which it was, than a long-term commitment."

Three years later, however, Jacqueline and Andrew were living together. By then, Jacqueline wanted to get married, but there she was, still with the same unsuitable—and as it turned out, still unfaithful—man. "I had always suspected he hadn't been one hundred percent faithful, but it became painfully clear when I answered the phone one afternoon and it was one of his relatives who had never met me. The caller inquired, 'Is this Kathleen?' I said, 'No, this is not. This is Jacqueline!'

"I got off the phone, locked myself in the bedroom, and wouldn't let Andrew in. In fact, I confronted him through the closed door. He confirmed my suspicions, saying, 'I guess I'm not meant to be with one person.' Total snake! He later on married the other woman, but I know he's cheated on her, too, because he tried to seduce me after we broke up!" The moral to Jacqueline's story? "Always follow your instincts where men are concerned."

If you stayed with a man who treated you badly, you need to look at your reasons. What drew you to a man like that? Rather than blaming everything on your ex, work on you. Yes, he's got problems, but it doesn't help you to try to figure out how to solve them. Instead, you should be concentrating on why you responded to his behavior the way you did.

That way, you can keep what happened with this man in mind for the next guy you get involved with. "What were the things he told you that you chose not to listen to—about him, you, or the relationship itself?" asks Hillyer. "So often in the beginning, he spills it all: 'I just want to have a good time; I don't want to get married.' Listen to what the guy is saying! You should also listen to what he says about his past relationships, because the problems he had in those relationships will probably recur in yours. Don't think, 'Oh, he just hasn't been with the right woman yet.'"

Leigh, age 25, made that mistake with Anthony. "When I started dating him, it was a casual thing, but after a month, we started getting more physically and emotionally involved. Still, throughout the whole relationship, he was very honest. He told me he didn't want to get into anything serious. He told me his last girlfriend had pressured him to get married, and he didn't want to get too heavy with me. He saw being committed as having to report to someone and being tied down. I knew all this from the outset, yet I still pursued him.

"We had been been dating for four or five months when we planned a trip to Puerto Rico. At the last minute he decided not to go, saying it wouldn't be fair to me because taking this trip would be a big step. That should have been a major sign. But then he changed his mind, and we went anyway. It was a good time, but nonetheless, about a month later, he broke up with me because he was afraid to commit.

"However, he wanted to continue to see me and have a 'nonemotional, physical relationship.' I went along with that for a while. But eventually I wanted to find someone who shared the same values as I did. Looking back, I see that there were definite warning signs. He told me straight up he wasn't into commitment, but I chose to be with him anyway. And sure enough, that's what ended up breaking us up."

Even if he's not coming right out and telling you he's bad news, you can often read between the lines. Debbie, age 28, wishes she had done just that with Jack, age 37. "Jack and I broke up because he felt he couldn't get married, although he had been married once before. In fact, Jack was still married when I first started dating him. Although he and his wife had been physically separated, it took him a long time to make that separation legal. That definitely should have been a warning sign. There was unfinished business from his last relationship that just never got finished. Even though he eventually got divorced, he never dealt with it in full. I should have steered clear of him."

Instead, they dated for six years and eventually got engaged, though Jack never talked about the wedding. In fact, they were about to move into a new apartment together when he realized he couldn't go through with their plans. He broke it off, but Debbie still believed there was hope. "He kept saying things like, 'You are the gift to the world, and I am everything dark.' But he wasn't willing to go into therapy, either as a couple or alone, which I think is very telling.

"I wish I'd had the strength to break up with him first—and I wish I had done it a long time ago." It's only now that Debbie's coming to conclusions she feels she should have reached years ago. "I think Jack is commitment-phobic. About a month after he broke it off, he told me he was seeing someone else. This woman just ended a five-year, live-in lesbian relationship with somebody who was suicidal, an alcoholic, and God knows what else. This is clearly an escape for Jack. She offers no threat of commitment whatsoever. He's just jumping into yet another new relationship without dealing with the issues from his last one—just as he did with me.

"What I'm working on now in therapy is why I would choose someone who is obviously not well suited for me. I'm embarrassed to talk about it. I feel manipulated and used. I had pegged Jack correctly a couple of months after we started going out, writing in my journal about possible problems he might have. I had definitely seen the signs. From now on, I'll trust my gut instinct."

When you think about the part you played in your breakup, don't get caught up in self-blame. Instead, approach the breakup from a learning perspective; just feeling guilty does you no good. "If you feel like a fool, okay, maybe you were a fool," admits Dr. Peterson. "Who hasn't been? You made a mistake and you move on. You're not perfect. You can't beat yourself up for it because not letting go of the mistake is just another mistake! You should also realize that maybe it wasn't a mistake at the time. Maybe you needed to be with him for a reason. Was there something you needed to learn from him to move on to the next relationship, which could be The One?"

Figuring Out Your Patterns

Now that you've started to ponder where you and your ex got off track, you're ready to tackle some of the issues that were at work in that relationship—and the ones that preceded it. Do this when you're not feeling too emotional; in order to get the most out of it, you need to be thinking rationally.

Although it can be difficult to relive painful memories, the questions below should help you identify your relationship patterns. Recognizing these patterns is the first step to building better relationships in the future. First, respond to all the questions with your most recent ex in mind. Plan to spend a good hour or more thinking about the questions and writing down your answers. (Writing everything down will help you clarify your thoughts.) Then set it aside. Later, go back and write down your responses for each previous boyfriend. Keep your notes in your journal so they're all in one place.

1. Were you attracted to him initially? Why or why not?
2. If you weren't impressed by him right away, what eventually won you over?
3. How did your feelings toward him change over the course of the relationship?
4. Could you be yourself around him?
5. Did you try to change him? Did he try to change you? How?
6. If there was a problem, did you feel able to discuss it with him? Why or why not?
7. What did you like most about him? What did you like least?
8. When you first became involved with him, did you have any qualms? What were they?
9. Were there any turning points in your relationship? If so, what were they?
10. What did you want from this relationship?
11. How honest were you with him? How honest was he with you?
12. Did you ever feel guilty while you were dating him? If so, about what?
13. Did you have a life outside of each other while you were in the relationship?
14. What were your biggest fights about?

What Went Wrong

15. What were the major issues that led to the breakup?
16. What did you do to contribute to the demise of the relationship?
17. What was missing in this relationship that you're determined to get next time around?
18. Which of the following describes him?

emotionally unavailable B

made promises he didn't keep

commitment phobic

pressured you to marry him

(too young) B

too old

(controlling)

too passive

lied a lot

(selfish)

abused drugs or alcohol B

compulsive gambler

physically abusive

mentally abusive

didn't get along with his family

disliked by your friends and family

married

gay

(depended on you too much)

couldn't hold a job

unreliable

philandering

(always wanted to have sex)

never wanted to have sex

always borrowed money

lived beyond his means

partied a lot with his buddies B

didn't have any close friends

didn't respect you

(jealous)

cheap	*rarely took you on dates*
criticized you a lot	*never finished anything he started*
underachiever	*workaholic*

After you've answered all these questions for each of your past relationships, compare your responses. What qualities do your ex-boyfriends share? How was your behavior similar from relationship to relationship? What conclusions can you draw from these similarities?

Avoiding Mr. Wrong

It's easy to get caught up in a cycle of continually dating and breaking up with the same type, even if he's all wrong for you. Maybe you have a wallet-sized picture in your head of exactly what the man of your dreams looks like—plus info on his job, what cologne he wears, and whether he likes his shrimp with cocktail or tartar sauce. But think about what you might be missing. In what ways is your type limiting? What do you give up by sticking to it? You should also consider the ways in which consistently going for a certain type can actually be destructive. If you only pay attention to certain physical features or personality traits, what negative qualities might you be overlooking?

Do you always gravitate toward the same type of guy? There are far too many types to list them all here, but you may recognize one (or more) of these:

- **The Strong, Silent, and Uncommunicative Type**

"I used to think the most important thing was that the person I dated was kind of that James Dean personality," says Robin, age 24. "But deep and brooding is not all it's cracked up to be. Aaron's way of dealing with problems was to shut down. Unfortunately, loners don't always make the best boyfriends.

"Now I realize that the person you date should be your best friend—and you should be able to talk to him about everything. I'm looking for a guy who is able to communicate problems, concerns, and issues—and cares enough about me to want to work through them rather than make decisions on his own and inform me of them later. Communication is key."

- **Mr. Selfish**

"Most of the men I've been involved with have been remarkably self-absorbed," says Amelia, age 27. "After Andy and I moved in together, for example, he would go out with friends until two in the morning without telling me beforehand. He never hung out with my friends; he started to ignore me in social situations. After a year, it got to the point where people were telling me I was masochistic to be in a relationship with him. After our breakup, I continued to sleep with him for another year, nurturing fantasies of a reconciliation. When I found out he'd had a girlfriend for six months but never told me, I blew up, since we'd had sex in that time. He'd felt it was none of my business.

"Familiarity goes a long way in relationships, and unfortunately, what's familiar to me is adversity. I've had boyfriends borrow money from me and then not repay it, sleep with me and then not call, and tell me in detail about other women they are interested in. What drew me to these guys in the first place? We're all afraid of tedium. When I'm with someone who I know won't be boring, it's attractive even if I know I'll be stepped on or used. I'm motivated by a desire to feel dynamic, interesting, challenged, and alive. While I'm still looking for someone stimulating, now I'm less ready to excuse unacceptable behavior. I'm learning that guys don't have to be bastards to be exciting."

- **The Hunk**

"I go for the Antonio Banderas type—hot, long hair, bad boy," says Laura, age 25. "All the guys I like look like my first boyfriend. If he's any other type, he can forget it. I want people to notice my guy and think he's cool. I always want the wild ones who aren't ready to settle down anytime soon. The draw is that they offer me a sense of adventure, fun, and excitement. But a lot of the attraction is just physical.

"Deep down, I know looks aren't everything. I have been dating a hot guy in a band for three years, but he's still never called me his girlfriend. He doesn't want any ties. But I think a big reason I stay is because I'm trying to recreate my relationship with my first boyfriend with someone much like him. I am working on figuring out why I let myself get taken advantage of."

- **The Controller**

    "I had always dated men who were very controlling," says Rhonda, age 32. "They would tell me what to do and how to do it, on everything from what to cook for dinner to what to wear to the movies. But my mother is very meek and her boyfriends always controlled her, so I just thought it was normal. After I broke up with my last serious boyfriend, I realized I was sick of being treated like I had no mind of my own and made a conscious decision not to go for guys like that anymore. I took a break from dating and really tried to think about why I allowed myself to be treated like that when I obviously deserve better.

    "Being controlled made me feel loved, but it's really a sign of total disrespect. When I felt ready to start dating again, I promised myself that if a guy told me what to do, I would tell *him* what to do—leave! And so far I have dated several nice guys who value me and don't push me around. There are nice guys out there."

- **The Emotional Evader**

    "I have repeatedly dated unavailable men," says Darcy, age 23. "My two long-term boyfriends both told me they couldn't fall in love with me—that they couldn't love anybody. I just figured that eventually I would make them see the light. I didn't want to see these guys as distant. I chose, instead, to consider them 'macho,' convincing myself they were hiding their feelings and at some point I'd see their true emotions.

    "My father smoked a lot of pot when I was

a kid, and even though he was around physically, he now admits he was 'never really there.' Maybe this is why an unavailable guy appeals to me. Since my last big breakup, I've dated a couple of guys, but one was engaged to someone else and one was still in love with his ex-girlfriend. I'm now looking for someone more sensitive and more emotional. I'm working on figuring out why I like the guys I do and starting to change."

The Worst Kind of Mr. Wrong: The Abuser

"Three months after Brian and I started dating, we moved in together and got two kittens," remembers Jenni, age 25. "One night, while we were having a fight, Brian picked up one of the kittens, looked me in the eye, told me to shut up, and rammed the kitten's head into the wall—hard, not just a tap. I knew he did it to hurt me. The kitten went limp, and I got hysterical, begging Brian to give it to me so I could take it to the hospital. He said if I didn't shut up, he'd kill it. He told me to leave it alone, claiming it would be okay in the morning. I took it to the vet the next day, and it turned out the kitten had brain hemorrhaging and severe brain damage.

"Two other cats I had had also died under questionable circumstances. I don't like to think about what happened to them. Brian was so jealous of the cats. He told me I loved the cats more than I loved him. I was so trusting. I couldn't believe anyone could hurt a helpless animal."

But Jenni didn't leave. "I was in denial, not

wanting to believe anything bad about this guy I loved. I was committed to the relationship and wanted it to work out. Since my parents knew we lived together, it was expected that we would get married. And even though Brian was violent at times, he would always be so apologetic and loving afterward."

In fact, as the relationship progressed, Jenni became more and more blinded by Brian's sweet side. "Before Brian went to visit his parents at Christmas, we had been having problems and thinking about breaking up. Brian had taken away a lot of my personal privileges—I wasn't allowed to have a pet to love, I wasn't allowed friends, I wasn't allowed to use the phone. But, unbelievably, we had been fighting over commitment: I wanted a ring.

"The day he was supposed to come back from his parents, his ex-girlfriend called, and I freaked. We had had some problems before with another girl calling, so we got an unlisted number and agreed not to give it out to exes. I suspected he had seen this girl when he was at his parents' and was really angry. When he got home, we had a huge argument about it, and he slept on the couch.

"The next day, when I got home from work, we had an even worse fight about the call. He grabbed me and threw me on the couch. He'd always push me and throw me around, but I never thought it was abuse because he didn't hit me. I ran down the hall, and he picked me up, holding me against the wall with his hand around my neck. I was being choked, my feet dangling off the ground, and the whole time I thought, 'Oh, my God, he's going to accidentally hurt me.' No lie—I really didn't think he would knowingly do anything to me. Then he threw me across the room, and I hit the wall. That's the first time I thought, 'He could hurt me, he could kill me, he's not stopping.' I'm sure this is how Nicole Brown Simpson felt.

"I thought he was going to paralyze me or break my neck. He pushed me down and started choking me. He had me down on the floor, holding me by the neck, when he raised his hand to punch me, full fist. I knew it was coming, and I knew I was dead. But then he just let me go, calm as day, and got up and walked away. I grabbed my purse and hightailed it out of there. He ran to the door and yelled, 'Yeah, run, Jenni, run.' The next day, I moved out.

"Brian and I could relate on the level that we'd both been abused as children. But the problem was, I was trying to break my cycle and he wasn't. He always said he never wanted to turn into his dad, but he acted exactly like him. I just never thought he would hurt me."

Unfortunately, according to the National Council on Child Abuse and Family Violence, a woman is abused every twelve seconds by her partner. If you, like Jenni, were abused, pat yourself on the back for no longer being part of that statistic. It takes a lot of guts to break away from an abusive situation, and you did it. "Congratulate yourself," says Dr. Judy. "You should feel fantastic that you've gotten out of the pattern."

But don't break out the bubbly just yet—there's a long road ahead. While you're probably glad in many ways to be free of him, you may also be a little confused. Do you miss his kisses, even though you still have bruises he inflicted? You might feel guilty about feeling this way about a guy who caused you so much pain, but it's not surprising that you miss someone you cared about. Besides, as Dr. Judy explains, "you're not really longing for the person who abused you—you're longing to change him."

Figuring out what attracted you to him and why you put up with his abuse in the first place is an important step. Was he charming and adoring at first, not showing his true colors until you were already sucked in? Did he continually promise you that he was sorry, that he loved you, that it would never happen again? Did you frequently make excuses to yourself and others for his behavior? Did you blame yourself? Dr. Mojas explains, "It's easy for an abused woman to take on the blame, even when she knows she doesn't deserve to be beaten because she doesn't have dinner ready. When her partner says it's a sign of disrespecting him, she believes that on some level. She takes too much responsibility. And since an abuser doesn't take any responsibility for his behavior, who better for him to be with? He thinks he's not really to blame because the woman 'made' him do it.

"When a woman meets an abuser, there's an intense honeymoon period with flowers and candy, then a slow buildup of tension. He projects onto her that she's victimizing him, and then there's an explosion and finally the makeup period. She's constantly trying to be good enough to get the nice treatment. That's why she stays."

Catherine, age 29, was caught in that vicious

cycle for nearly four years. Although her ex never physically hurt her, he caused her plenty of mental torment. "I knew Ben was no good for me. He could be so confrontational and emotional. Once, a guy at work was attracted to me, and I didn't like it. Then one day he called in sick. I found out later that Ben had sent someone to knock him around a little. He was into ridiculous acts of passion."

After Ben moved in with her, Catherine became obsessed with a locked box he kept in her bedroom. "I thought about going to the fire station up the road to get an ax so I could get into it. One day I got some knives from the kitchen and pried it open." A few months earlier, Catherine had been diagnosed with chlamydia and genital warts. Now she knew why. "The box was full of pictures of other girls going through my vanity and lying on my bed. I felt sick. I couldn't shake it. He had always denied seeing other women, but here were these photos. He was a pathological liar—it was shocking.

"But even though he'd done all these awful things, he was always dangling a carrot. He was at my beck and call. I'd ask him to bring me lunch, and he'd be there. He'd buy me jewelry. I worked nights, and he'd pick me up. He took care of me all the time. And he was a great lover."

However, as the bad times built up, Catherine began to realize she was in too deep. "One day I thought, 'How do I get rid of this parasite? I've got to throw the hairdryer in his bath.' I didn't do it, but I know what it feels like to be on the brink of insanity. I knew Ben loved me and that I was the best thing he ever had. He would tell me that and cry! What I could never understand was how he could love me and do these things to me.

"I finally broke up with him and got a restraining order against him, but eight months later, I foolishly slept with him again. After that, he wouldn't leave me alone. I finally had to move overseas to get away from him."

Even though you, too, have now gotten out of your situation, you need to evaluate your past relationships in order to learn the root of your patterns and to avoid getting involved with another abuser in the future. Says Dr. Judy, "The reason you were so attached to him had nothing to do with that particular person. Maybe you were abused in your past. People always think it's their fault they were abused, but it's not."

What experiences have made you allow yourself to be treated this way? You can't answer that on your own. "Research indicates that talking about your experience and expressing your emotions as soon as possible are the primary keys to recovery," says Lynne Finney, J.D., M.S.W., in her book *Reach for Joy: How to Find the Right Therapist and Therapy for You* (The Crossing Press, Inc., 1995). Trying to put the abuse out of your mind so you can just get on with your life is a serious mistake. According to Finney, "Although you may think you can get through it by yourself, you will suffer the effects for many years unless you can talk about what happened and ask for help."

Find an individual therapist, or call the National Family Violence Helpline at 1-800-222-2000 for a referral to an organization or support group in your area. Jenni, age 25, explains, "Therapy has helped me see the situation for what it was. I've come to terms with myself. I never want to go back to being in a relationship like that. Now I always want to go forward." If you don't deal with your issues now, you're much more likely to get into another abusive situation in the future. Don't take the risk.

What You're Like in a Relationship

Although you may not be completely aware of it, you probably tend to act a certain way toward men you get into relationships with, partly as a result of the guys you choose and partly as a result of your own personal issues. It's not easy to change after relying on the same behavior for a lifetime, especially since you may have several areas you need to work on. But when your patterns aren't productive, it simply doesn't make sense to keep falling back on them.

Having trouble recognizing the role you play in a relationship? Here are a few that might ring a bell:

- **The Handywoman**
"I seek men who need help," says Missy, age 27. "I'm a nurturing type of person; I like being the one to help them through stuff. Jon was always going into cycles where one minute everything would be great and the next he'd feel like he was a loser and just wanted to keep to himself. I always said I'd give him his space and help him get through the bad times. But it was a one-way street. I was never top priority in his

life. Up till then, I'd dated a lot of guys like that. But finally, Jon got me to the point where I felt I would never help another person again.

"For a while I thought, 'I should have done this' or 'I shouldn't have done that.' Like when I would complain that he didn't call when he said he would, it would set him off and he'd turn it around to make me feel guilty for bringing it up. But I still thought I should have been able to help him. It was only when I started dating Bruce that I realized it wasn't my fault. I didn't have to be with someone like Jon. Bruce helped me see that there were loving, supportive, sensitive people out there who are already mentally stable and ready for a relationship."

- **The Chameleon**

"I'd always wanted to be whatever men wanted me to be, especially in the bedroom," admits Lizzie, age 31. "I'd try to meet their wildest expectations so they'd think I was the best woman they'd ever been with. I didn't even realize I was like this until one night when I picked up this guy at a bar and had a really lousy one-night stand. I thought, 'This isn't working. . . . I can't do this anymore.' Sex had lost all meaning for me.

"For three years after that incident, I was celibate and didn't date anyone at all. During that time, I thought a lot about my issues. I realized I wanted to have a healthy relationship instead of doing everything to please the guy and throwing my identity out the window. I think my behavior had a lot to do with a need for approval. My current boyfriend is the first guy

I have actually been myself around. I think I have finally learned that myself is more than enough."

- **The Distancer**

"I have always distanced myself from boyfriends," says Ivy, age 27. "I think it's because I don't trust anyone. I do it as soon as I feel close to somebody and realize he has the power to hurt me. I know that at some point I am going to have to trust this person if I want it to go further, but I just choose not to. I'll go from that initial period of spending all my time with him to saying I have to work on weekends or that I want to be alone during the week.

"I go backward instead of forward. It's a gradual process. I went from seeing my last boyfriend five nights a week to seeing him only on weekends nine months into the relationship. I'd say, 'Isn't this fun? It's good to miss each other sometimes,' when really I just wanted to get away from him. Because my parents weren't always honest with me when I was young, I've always had a hard time trusting them; I guess that's partly what this pattern stems from. With my new boyfriend, I have promised myself that when I feel this way, I am going to fight through being uncomfortable for a while rather than running away."

- **The Doormat**

"When I was dating Tyler, this really hot guy everyone was after, I totally set aside my own needs," remembers Gail, age 24. "If he made me mad, I wouldn't say anything. I wanted everything to be perfect between us, even if that meant not speaking up when something was wrong. I'm pretty easygoing anyway, but this was me times ten. The person I was with my friends and the person I was in this relationship were like two different people.

"He'd do these really disrespectful things to me and I'd just make excuses for him. But the last straw came when I was in the hospital for ten days and he didn't come visit me. I dumped him and decided that, from then on, I came first, and I was never going to let anybody treat me badly again. With my next boyfriend, I voiced my opinions and was the strong woman I had always been outside of my old relationship."

- **The Boss**

"I definitely tell boyfriends my opinion on how they should do things," says Jayna, age 22. "I was raised to be a take-charge kind of person. So if a boyfriend is just sitting back, I'll take over. I like to fix situations, so I have no problems telling guys what to do and how to do it—and if the guys don't follow my advice, I get pissed. Guys have broken up with me before because I'm too bossy.

"My current boyfriend sometimes tells me, 'Let me be in control for once. You need to let me do this.' My first reaction is that he won't be able to get things done unless I help out. But I am trying to chill on the nagging. I know that telling him what to do is doing nothing for me. He needs to make his own decisions. I'm keeping my mouth shut more and avoiding situations where I'm tempted to give him advice. It's frustrating to keep quiet, but I know I need to be his girlfriend instead of his mom."

Why Am I Like This?

Your patterns stem from your past experiences, starting with your relationship with your parents. What did your parents teach you about love? What was your childhood like? Are there issues between you and your parents or other childhood role models that you're subconsciously trying to work out through your relationships with men? If you didn't get along well with one or both of your parents, you may have once sworn you would never be like them. But it's difficult to escape their influence. Whether you like it or not, your past probably plays a powerful role in shaping your present.

Ivy, age 27, for example, sees herself acting out her mother's behavior. "When I was growing up, my mother got engaged twice—and broke it off both times. I used to think she just loved to fall in love, but now I see that she has problems getting close to people. So do I. I now realize the way I pull away in relationships is exactly how my mom has always pulled away from people—including me."

Brenda, age 27, never felt close to her dad, but she ended up choosing someone very similar to him for a boyfriend. "Eddie was a lot like my father, which is probably why I fell in love with him—even though it's not good, it's familiar. They're both very selfish and controlling. But reliving the dysfunctional relationship I had with my dad has been very painful."

Suppose you, like Brenda, have a parent or someone else in your past who was very domineering. "You could end up in a relationship with someone who's also powerful and controlling," says Dr. Mojas, "or you could get involved with a guy who's passive and find yourself becoming controlling. The pain from your past leads to patterns that come up and cause pain again; you recreate the original painful situation so you can 'fix' it this time. There's a tendency to think the only love that's worth getting is the love that's hard to get."

Dr. Lutwin has seen this frequently in his twenty-eight years of practice. "For example, one patient of mine kept going out with guys with substance-abuse problems. Her father was an alcoholic, and she was trying to relive her relationship with him by having a positive relationship with another substance abuser. If you haven't done your homework and looked at your self-destructive patterns, you'll just keep going after these same wrong men. But if you develop self-knowledge, you can put checks and balances on this behavior. You can tell yourself, 'I don't need to seek out men like this to try to get the approval that will finally put to rest my problems with my dad.'" Because it just doesn't work that way.

His Patterns

As you think about the reasons your relationship broke down, you may notice that he has his patterns, too. Maybe he would prefer someone to attend to his every whim instead of building a relationship between equals. Maybe he would rather jump from affair to affair for the rest of his born days instead of ever settling down for a commitment.

However, this isn't your concern anymore. Whatever his patterns are, you shouldn't waste your time worrying about how to help him work through them. Instead, recognize that your breakup may have had more to do with your ex trying to cope with his own problems than with his rejecting you as a person. You may well watch him go on to wreck all his future relationships too. Take consolation in the fact that being on your own or with someone else could make you much happier.

Ultimately, maybe you and your ex just weren't meant to be. "Sometimes the guys we get involved with are practice," says Hillyer. "Maybe you needed to work that issue out—and maybe he had an issue he needed to work out, too. We get drawn to people for reasons. That may have been all the relationship was about, but it can be a good thing."

So rather than analyze the roots of *his* behavior, think about how it affected *yours*. Why did you respond in the ways you did? What did he bring out in you that might be problematic? Understanding your reactions to your ex's behavior can help you form healthier future relationships. Every guy has patterns, but it's up to you to decide what you can't live with—and now you're better equipped to do so.

How Do I Change?

Now that you've thought about your part in the breakup, asked your friends' opinions, put your past relationships to the test, and analyzed your behavior, you can probably see certain trends emerging. The next step is to review what you've discovered, then decide on a positive plan for your future.

"Mark was a pathological liar," says Nancy, age 27. "He was my college professor, and every girl in class had a crush on him. I was coming off an ugly-duckling complex and was flattered he had chosen me. Little did I know that he was also dating three other women in the class. In fact, I later found out a classmate *lived* with him for two weeks of our relationship! But the final straw came when he told me he had to go home one night to work on a paper, and I spied on him in the pool hall making out with another woman. You can dismiss certain lies, but to see one of them in action is devastating. It snapped me into action, and I broke up with him.

"I probably caught Mark in twenty lies while we were dating, but I thought if I could just be good enough, I could change him by example. I worked at our relationship for a year and a half, but I found that when you're a liar at heart, you really can't change."

This wasn't the first time Nancy had gotten involved with someone like Mark. Her first boyfriend, Robby, also lied about things, including the fact that he was gay. "My pattern probably goes back to my estranged dad," says Nancy.

"With him, there's always been a series of lies. I distinctly remember my sister and me dressed up in our finest outfits, waiting for Dad to come take us Christmas shopping when we were little kids. We sat there all day long, and he never came. The whole rest of my life has been like that with him. He'll say, 'I'll call. I'll come by,' but it never happens. I was raised by women, and my only male influence was full of broken promises."

Finally, Nancy realized she needed to break her cycle. "Two and a half years ago, I made a radical change. I went to the bookstore and read every relationship book I could get my hands on to learn how to do it right. I got some great advice and discovered I had a pattern of not liking nice guys. After a lot of hard work, I felt I was ready for the right relationship at last. Then I started dating Gordon, and we've been together ever since. With him, I knew what I wanted, and I got it. You get what you ask for. I was so used to asking for jerks—but I'll never make that mistake again."

Once you, like Nancy, have figured out where your relationship went wrong, make a conscious effort to determine why it didn't work and how you'll alter your actions in the future. Before you dismiss a suitor as unsuitable, think about what you're looking for now, not what you've looked for in the past. And before you fall into the same bad habits, concentrate on how you'll do things differently this time around. If you change for the better, so will your future relationships.

Breaking Negative Patterns

Ready for a fresh start? First, try this: "Think of the best friend you've ever had, then write down that person's qualities and characteristics," says Childs. "Then think of a good acquaintance—someone you play tennis with or go out to dinner with sometimes—and write down that person's qualities. Next, write down the qualities of a person you tolerate. Then write down the qualities of someone who makes you uncomfortable. And finally, write down the qualities of someone who's been a destructive and poisonous person in your life." Now see which category best describes your exes. If you find it's the final one, it's no surprise to Childs. As she puts it, "Many people choose life mates they wouldn't choose as enemies!"

If you're not happy with your choices, make a commitment to make better decisions in the future. That means giving yourself the freedom to abandon destructive patterns instead of continuing to try harder to make relationships work within them. "We tend to do the same thing over and over again, so improving usually means doing that same thing better and better," Hillyer explains. "If you have a pattern of taking care of deadbeat guys, for example, you might think, 'I'm going to take even better care of this guy than I already am,' and then feel you're improving as a person as a result—that's how we're conditioned. You force yourself to put more effort into the situation and push yourself to the limit, just like you might do in your career or in a sport.

But to improve upon a bad pattern, you have to rid yourself of it and replace it with a positive one."

If you're trying to break a bad pattern, "talking to yourself is one of the most effective and valuable techniques," says Hillyer. "Start repeating positive statements in your mind, like 'I'm capable of change,' 'It's my life,' or 'I have control.' Eventually, they'll replace negative statements like 'I'm helpless,' 'I can't,' or 'Nothing ever changes.' If you stay with it, you can actually reprogram your brain."

Hillyer suggests trying the following three-step exercise:

1. Recognize old negative, self-defeating thoughts like "He's not going to care about me" or "I always end up with the same kind of guys."
2. Stop the thoughts by saying to yourself "No!" or "Get out of my head!" (See page 128 for more help on this.)
3. Replace it with your positive "I can," "I am," "I'm capable," "I'm lovable," or "I deserve better" statement. "One statement you might try is 'I am ready and open for a relationship with a loving and healthy man,' or 'I deserve a wonderful, nurturing relationship,'" says Hillyer. "But be sure to keep it positive. 'I won't date alcoholics anymore' would not be the way to go, since it's not a positive statement."

You may end up doing this fifty to one hundred times a day, but it will only take a few

What Went Wrong

minutes—and before long, you'll notice the shift. Positive thoughts automatically take over, just like the negative ones take over now. "We don't have to think about negative thoughts for them to come into our heads, do we?" Hillyer points out. "Well, the same applies for positive ones."

Another way to start breaking bad patterns is to look in the mirror and say, "I love you. I really love you." According to Dr. Cooper, you should do that every day and as often as you can—while you're putting on makeup, brushing your teeth, whatever. "You need to build up your own self-love—literally," says Dr. Cooper. "If you do this exercise religiously, you will notice a real difference in your self-esteem after thirty days. It sounds corny, but it's tremendously effective."

You may also want to try displaying a particularly cute childhood photo of yourself on your mirror, car dashboard, or desk—anywhere it can't be missed. Look at the picture every day and ask yourself "How would I like this child to be treated by my boyfriend?" No doubt you'd want her to be loved, valued, and respected. When you're dating a new guy who does something that brings to mind old patterns, pull up the pic in your mind. Your first impulse, naturally, is to protect that child from being hurt. Now transfer that impulse to the grown-up version of that child—that is, you as you are today. You are no less deserving of love, value, and respect than you were the day that photo was taken, and you owe it to yourself not to tolerate anything less.

These exercises work because they help you make lasting changes in yourself. According to

Childs, "If you have to make a conscious effort out of a sense of obligation to try someone new, it doesn't work. You can't say, 'Okay, I think I'll try a nice, nerdy guy now.' Instead, it has to be an internal shift from within. Changes don't come from just saying 'Oh, I refuse to be treated badly anymore.' At some point, you have to say 'This won't happen again,' and then work on making *sure* it doesn't. That means developing a sense of self-esteem and learning to value and take care of yourself. Eat right, do meditation, exercise—work on a lifestyle where you feel better about yourself. If you can't get the affirmation you need from your friends or family, turn to a support group or therapist. Make a habit of taking responsibility for yourself—and taking care of yourself. When it comes to adults, there are no victims. You do have choices."

And you ought to take those choices seriously. "People spend more time looking for a car than for a mate," Childs laments. "But if you can decide what kind of car you want, why couldn't you do the same for a man? If you want a foreign car, you wouldn't go into the Ford dealership, would you? You've got to know what you want, or you'll never get it." That's why Childs recommends you make a checklist of things you can't live with and things you can't live without in a relationship. What are you looking for? What do you want to avoid? Write it down. That way, you have to pin down what you want—and what you don't. Now, when you're thinking about a possible date, you'll have something to go by besides how he looks or what he does for a living. A guy could have a great smile and a fat paycheck and not care about you one bit. Instead, look for values that are important to you—like honesty or good communication skills, for example. Think about the things you wrote down about your best friend in the list you made earlier of people's characteristics, and go from there. Remember, the most important thing in a relationship is friendship.

What If I Can't Seem to Change?

If you feel you can't objectively analyze your past relationships or make positive changes for your future on your own, seeking the help of someone trained in dealing with such situations is a healthy step. "If you've ever thought about getting into therapy, after a breakup is probably a good time to go," says Dr. Mojas. "Most people don't have the motivation to spend the time and money to change patterns during a good time. And when you're in pain, that's when you'll grow the most."

Remember, it's okay to get help. "When Joshua broke up with me, I was dealing with a lot of feelings and thought about seeing a therapist," says Lana, age 23. "But I would have been too embarrassed. I wouldn't have wanted my mom to know I was going, so I didn't pursue it."

If you, like Lana, feel uncomfortable about going to therapy, keep in mind that seeking help doesn't mean you're crazy. On the contrary, it shows that you're healthy enough to want to make positive changes in your life. Repressing or denying your feelings would be much, much worse.

Your breakup may have triggered emotions you've repressed about past losses. Were your parents divorced when you were little? Did your family move around a lot? Have you recently lost your job? Has someone close to you died? All these losses could be affecting how you're handling your breakup, and you may not be able to handle the repercussions from them on your own. Facing your feelings might be painful, but if you don't confront them they'll just keep growing and growing and growing.

Truth is, anyone can benefit from therapy. But you should definitely go if you've been experiencing significant disturbances in sleep or appetite, have lost interest in activities you used to enjoy, or have been feeling worthless, hopeless, or overwhelmingly lethargic or upset for more than a few weeks. These are all signs from your brain saying, "I need help!" If you are suicidal or have been abused, therapy is a must; you should not attempt to handle those issues on your own.

Why Can't My Best Friend Be My Therapist?

Talking to your pals about your breakup can be very therapeutic, and it's certainly not a bad thing to express your feelings. But since friends care about you so much, it might be impossible for them to be completely unbiased or to devote their full attention to your problem for the length of time you need to work through your emotions. Furthermore, if you're really depressed, they're probably not equipped to handle some of the issues that might come up.

"Talking to a friend can be very valuable if it seems to be helping you move ahead instead of being just a bitching session that's holding you back," says Hillyer. "But I'm a great believer in therapy. A friend can't be totally objective. Her own stuff is going to come up, which could taint her advice."

So while talking to pals can be a good thing, it's no substitute for professional help. Friends can help you to a point, but they can only do so much.

How Will I Ever Afford Therapy?

If you don't think you have the cash to cover counseling, consider your spending habits. Do you go out for lunch every day? Why not brown-bag it for a while and spend the savings on your mental well-being? After all, you shouldn't scrimp on yourself and your happiness. And therapy doesn't have to cost a zillion dollars an hour, contrary to popular belief. Here are some cost-cutters to consider:

- **Insurance.** If you have health insurance, it probably covers a number of therapy sessions. Call your insurance company or look at your plan to find out if mental-health benefits are offered. "I didn't think I could afford therapy," says Melissa, age 33. "But then I called my insurance company and found out they covered sixty percent of the fee. After I started going, I realized no amount of money was too much to pay. The experience was invaluable."

- **Colleges and universities.** In-house counseling programs are a staple at most schools. If your college days are over, it might be worth looking into a night class to take advantage of this benefit.
- **Publicly funded mental-health programs.** If you're in a low income bracket, you may qualify for public aid, which could score you free or discounted therapy. Call your state mental-health association for information on these programs.
- **Sliding scale.** Many nonprofit organizations and even private practices offer a sliding-scale payment plan, which is based on your income and how much you can afford. Says Jenni, age 25, "I was in an entry-level job and didn't have mental-health coverage. But I found a therapist who offered a sliding scale, so I only had to pay fifteen dollars per session."
- **Support groups.** Although they're not led by a licensed therapist, support groups such as Codependents Anonymous can still be beneficial. Talking to others who've been in a situation similar to yours is often a comforting and positive experience.

Which Therapist Is for Me?

There are so many different kinds of counseling, determining what's right for you can be a confusing endeavor. Whether you choose a psychologist, psychiatrist, clinical social worker, psychiatric nurse, or any of the other types of therapists out there, the most important factor to consider is whether you like the person. "A therapist's discipline is not as important as your feeling about the therapist," says Louise Lipman, Ph.D., a certified social worker in private practice in New York City. "You might feel more comfortable with one type of therapy over another, but the individual relationship with the therapist is what's crucial. It affects the whole experience."

Wondering whether to choose a male or female therapist? Gender shouldn't really matter. But if you are worried that you might be attracted to a male therapist, or if you have been abused or are having trouble opening up to men after your breakup, you'll probably want to select a woman.

Should I Choose Group or Individual Therapy?

Group and individual counseling each has its pros and cons. In individual therapy, you will get more focused, intense treatment, since the spotlight is on you and only you. But it's usually more expensive, and you won't get the opportunity to bond with others who share your experience, as you would in a group.

Group therapy allows you to see for yourself that others are going through the same thing you are. But because you won't receive the attention that you would in individual treatment, it may take longer to work through your problem.

Choosing an Individual Therapist

Although you may be tempted to grab the Yellow Pages, that's one of the worst ways to find a therapist. Instead, ask around and do a little research. That way, you'll be most likely to find someone you really like and trust. Here's how to do it.

1. Ask your friends, family, and doctor if they could suggest anyone. (If you're embarrassed, don't be. Remember, you're putting yourself first now, and that's nothing to be ashamed of.) Then contact your local mental-health association, explain your situation, and ask if they could give you a referral.

   Various professional organizations, such as the American Association of Marriage and Family Counselors (909-621-4749), the American Medical Association (312-464-5000), and the American Psychological Association (202-336-5500) also make recommendations, as do many insurance carriers. If you call these referral services, you are usually given the name of the next therapist on the roster or the one closest to your area rather than the name of the therapist who might be best for you. If you act on these recommendations, be sure to double-check the person's credibility with someone else, as explained below.

2. Once you collect as many names as you possibly can, read over your list. Give priority to any names that appear more than once, or which were given to you by someone you

highly trust. Select a handful of therapists, and then check with your state licensing authority (look in the government listings of your local phone book) to see if your candidates have valid licenses and to find out if any disciplinary actions have been taken against them. If you receive negative information about anyone, strike that person from the list.

3. After you have narrowed your selections, call the therapists and ask how long they've been practicing; if they're licensed and, if so, by whom; what their education and background are; if they typically handle cases such as yours; and how much they charge. Eliminate anyone who would not answer your questions or was rude to you, but set up interviews with those who meet your qualifications. Be sure to ask if the therapist charges a consultation fee. Some do, but it's money well spent if it means finding the person who can best fit your needs.

4. For each interview, bring along a pad and pen to take notes on how the therapist responds to your questions and how you feel about him or her.

Usually, the first thing your potential therapist will ask is why you are seeking therapy. Explain that you're going through a breakup, touching on what led to it and how you're feeling now. Then you may find it helpful to ask some or all of the following questions from the list in Finney's *Reach for Joy: How to Find the Right Therapist and Therapy for You*:

- What do you think about what I've said?
- What would my treatment involve?
- What techniques would you use in my treatment?
- Do you give direction in your therapy or take a more passive role?
- How much time will my treatment require?
- What if I need to reach you in an emergency or ask you something between sessions?
- How much will this cost?
- Will my insurance at least partially cover this treatment or do you offer a sliding payment scale?

Before making your selection, consider how the candidate treated you and whether you liked him or her. It's a good idea to choose the one you have the most positive feeling about, even if he or she isn't the one with the best credentials. But even after you select someone, hold on to your notes. If you are unsatisfied with your therapist, you can always switch to your second choice at a later date.

Choosing a Therapy Group

To choose a group, follow the same tips for finding an individual therapist: Ask around, call referral services, and make a list of possible candidates. Usually, a group will require you to go through an interview process with the group leader before accepting you as a new member. In this interview, be sure to find out what the purpose of the group is, what types of techniques are used, and what is expected of you as a group member. Ask what the leader's educational background and qualifications are. After the interview, ask yourself if you feel comfortable with the group leader, if he or she respected you, and, most importantly, whether you liked the person or not.

Go with your gut feeling when selecting a group. If you like the leader and feel good about the group's goals, it is probably the right choice. But if not, don't worry—your decision is never irreversible.

6

Reinventing Yourself

Okay, so you're no longer so-and-so's girlfriend, nor are you his wife-to-be, the future mother of his children, the person building a cabin in the mountains with him for retirement, or even the one going to the Mariah Carey concert with him next week. Now you're just ... you. And maybe you're not even sure who that is anymore.

All the grand plans you made with him are suddenly null and void. No wonder you feel empty; you've got to start over. However, this breakup—painful though it may be—could catapult you into a period of tremendous personal growth. As the saying goes, what doesn't kill you makes you stronger.

Kim, age 23, found that out the hard way. "We kept in touch, and Kenny called and visited, but I was adamant that we would not get back together if he was going to cheat on me again. I ended up going abroad to Spain for the following semester, and though I missed Kenny very much, it was a blessing in disguise. He sent me letters with rose petals in them, but I didn't have to see him, so it gave me some perspective. He'd cheated on me numerous times, and he was a liar. Everything was like a soap opera with him. Being away, I realized I didn't need to be treated like that."

Living it up in Madrid, Kim was reborn as an independent, fun-loving woman. "Before leaving, I cut my long hair into a short bob—I felt liberated. In Spain, I made new friends and led an entirely different life doing incredible things. I got a huge surge of energy and regained my self-confidence. I'll never let anyone take advantage of me again."

Kim learned that she could enjoy life without Kenny and that, in fact, it could actually be better without him. While going through a breakup was tough for her, Kim came out of it a wiser and well-traveled woman—with easy-to-manage hair!

Like Kim, you're on your own now. Why not make the best of it? Take advantage of this time to explore new interests, boost your self-esteem, and focus on yourself. You could come out of this ordeal stronger, happier, and more fulfilled than ever! Here's how.

Take Action

"If all you can think about right now is Bobby, Bobby, Bobby, you need to shift the attention from him to *you*," advises Hillyer. "Often in relationships, we focus on what the other person wants. Now is the time to think about you and only you. Ask yourself: 'What do I need right now? What's good for me?' It might just be taking a walk or calling a sympathetic friend. But don't let yourself dwell on him."

Now's the time to think of yourself, so pursue whatever will make you happy. Enjoy your freedom of choice: Remember, you don't have to worry about what he thinks anymore. Make a list of everything you wanted to do with your ex that he wasn't into: Get a dog. Go dancing. Buy a new couch. Listen to music while falling asleep. Take a white-water rafting trip. No one's holding you back anymore, so whatever it is, go for it!

You can't control what your ex does or doesn't do, but you can control your reaction to it. Rather than getting down about the fact that he broke up with you, try to see it as an opportunity. Now you have more time and energy for you and what you want. Take a continuing-education class in something fun that you've always wanted to learn more about. Water-ski on weekends, wallpaper the bathroom, write a screenplay. All those things you've been meaning to get to someday? Someday is here.

I know what you're thinking. When people told me, "Hey! Now you've got time to pursue your own interests!" I thought, "Great. My only interest is in getting my old boyfriend back. Everything else is meaningless." But in retrospect, that attitude did nothing but hold me back. It was only when I started doing things for *me*—redecorating my apartment, hosting my first dinner party, planning a trip to San Francisco—that I stopped being so miserable and started being happy again. You'll never feel better if you don't get out there and try. Force yourself if you have to. You could end up pleasantly surprised.

Take it from Dr. Peterson. "Instead of waiting and waiting for your ex to call you, join a gym or take a photography class. Even if you're crying all the way there, get yourself back into the social scene. The worst thing that could happen would be that you'd meet a new girlfriend—or even another guy. Wouldn't that be terrible! If nothing else, doing something new will distract you. If you just carry on with your life as is, all you'll notice is the thing that's missing: him. Inertia can lead to depression if you're not careful."

Become a Social Butterfly

Get a date book and start filling it! The simple acts of making plans, getting ready, and going out will do wonders for your psyche.

Spend time with old friends and start making new ones. Seek out people to fill the holes your ex has left in your life. If you liked his brainy conversation, go for a drink after work with a smart colleague. If you liked his sense of humor, meet a funny friend for dinner. Whatever wonderful qualities your ex had to offer, he's not the only one on the planet who's got them. Find what you're looking for in others.

And don't be afraid to get close to people you trust. Sometimes it's hard to let yourself be vulnerable after a breakup; you don't want to get hurt a second time. But shutting yourself off from the world and building walls between you and everyone who cares about you is a mistake. You have to learn to depend on others again.

However, talking about your breakup 24/7 can also be a problem. "Get off the 'woe is me' kick," cautions Dr. Cooper. "Too many people wallow in their pain and set themselves up to be permanent victims. Don't overburden your friends with your pain, or you'll eat up their attention and push them away."

You should also be careful not to become bitter about the entire male gender. Men aren't all bad! Prove it to yourself by spending some quality time with your guy friends. Bonus: It's good practice for dating again—you can flirt a little and enjoy a man's company with no strings attached.

As Torry, age 28, puts it, "When you don't have a boyfriend, it sure is nice to have a guy friend to raise your self-esteem. After Dustin and I broke up, my friend Lee would always tell me how wonderful I was, which was a real ego boost, and assure me that another guy would come along soon. A few months later, when I moved into a new apartment building, I met my neighbor Seth, who was great to pal around with. He was good-looking and tons of fun to go dancing with—you almost didn't need 'the real thing.' Getting over the trauma of being alone was a lot easier thanks to my male buds!"

If you used to go out with your boyfriend and other couples every weekend, work on establishing closer friendships with unattached people. As Robin, age 24, can attest, spending time with coupled friends can be awfully hard at first. "I found it painful to hang out with friends who had serious relationships. Since I wasn't part of a couple anymore, it just didn't feel comfortable. I really had to expand my social circle after my breakup."

You'll also want to start spending more time with pals you knew before you started dating your ex. Seeing mutual friends (coupled or not) will probably be too difficult at first: You'll be tempted to talk about your ex, and they'll serve as a constant reminder of happier days with him.

Schedule things to do during the times you're most depressed. Are Friday nights especially difficult for you? Then don't stay home watching TV. Go out on the town instead. Do you wake up Sunday mornings feeling blue? Make brunch dates with all your buddies. You may surprise yourself and actually have fun!

On the morning of my last birthday, my ex informed me that although he still loved me, we weren't getting back together. I was so upset I spent the rest of the day in a terrible funk—until that night, when I met nine of my friends for dinner at one of my favorite restaurants. Everyone brought me lovely gifts; somebody even made a cake. Suddenly I was the center of attention. We sat outside and ate and drank and talked and laughed for hours. When it was time for dessert, they lit the candles and all sang "Happy Birthday."

I felt genuinely happy again. Here were people I really cared about, who obviously cared about me back. I didn't need James after all. Because of those few hours spent among close friends, it ended up being one of the best birthdays I've ever had.

Look Good, Feel Better

As tempting as it is to go out in a flannel shirt, sweat pants, a ponytail, and no makeup, don't. Putting on something nice and spending time on your hair and makeup in the morning can help you approach the world with a positive outlook: Knowing you look your best is a sure-fire mood lifter.

If you think you'd like a new outer image to go with your new inner image, consider a change. Go to the best department store in town and get a makeover. Try out a different fashion style. Cut your hair into a pixie do, or dye it platinum. Leigh, age 25: "I worked out a lot, cut my hair shoulder-length, started plucking my eyebrows thinner, and wore more defined lipstick. I changed my whole look. Everyone loved it!"

But be careful. Drastic changes are not for the faint of heart, as Melissa, age 33, explains. "After I broke up with my boyfriend in college, I shaved the sides of my head. It was a little longer on top, but it looked horrible. I just wanted to look different, but it didn't make me happy. Plus, it took forever to grow out. Even six months afterward, when my family came to my graduation, they were all like, 'What is up with your hair?!'"

Take a Vacation

A trip could be just the ticket now. Visit old friends you haven't seen in a while. Or head for a destination where you'll be busy most of the time. Go sightseeing, spelunking, skydiving....

But whatever you do, don't go anywhere you went with your ex! And don't take a cruise or a romantic holiday where all you have planned is lying on the beach—you'll just end up surrounded by happy couples.

Missy, age 27, trekked all the way to Alaska—solo, no less—to nurture her tortured soul. "Going to Alaska alone was the best thing I could have done after my breakup with Jon. Up to that point, I was a big basket case. I hadn't really talked to anyone about the breakup in depth. I was crying all the time and very upset, but trying to put on a happy face. Even though we were through, I still hoped Jon would call me and come back.

"Going away made me realize life could go on without him. The whole breakup made me feel like I had lost myself. There was this big void in my life after Jon and I split up, and I didn't feel right for months. I became this cynical, bitter person instead of a romantic at heart, and I didn't like it. But going on the trip by myself really helped. It was good to get away from everyone and be alone with my thoughts, meet other people on the tour, and enjoy myself instead of just thinking, 'Oh, I've lost the love of my life.'"

Moving On (Literally)

If you've been thinking about relocating anyway, now is a good time to do it. Your place holds a lot of memories of you and your ex—memories you might be better off forgetting, at least for now—and a new place signifies a new start. You could move a few doors down, or you could head for somewhere on the other side of the country: somewhere you have old friends, somewhere you once visited that you loved, or even somewhere you've just always dreamed about.

That's what Julie, age 25, did. "A big part of my decision to move to New York was Jason. I didn't feel I was totally over him, and I thought going somewhere new would help. There are only so many places to go in Oklahoma City, and it seemed I was always running into him there. Even though I was homesick at first in New York, I was concentrating on me rather than him. I found a waitressing job, an internship, new friends, a publisher for my first novel, and a new boyfriend. It was the best thing I could have done for myself."

Brenda, age 27, had a similar experience. "When Eddie and I broke up, I was living at home with my parents. But one day, I just packed up my car and left. I had always been close to my aunt, and she'd been pushing me to come down to D.C., so I decided to go stay with her until I could find my own place. I felt I just had to get out of New Jersey—and Eddie had a lot to do with that. It's definitely been a good thing for me."

With your ex no longer around, you won't be reminded of what you're missing—which will allow you to go forward faster. Although moving somewhere new does mean added stress, in the long run it may speed up the healing process because your daily life will include fewer ties to your past. Of course, it takes time and effort to find a new job, a new apartment, and new friends, but what else are you going to spend that time and effort on? Pining for your ex?

On the other hand, you should be sure you're doing it for the right reasons. If the breakup motivates you to move when you've been dreaming about it anyway, by all means, do it. But if you're only doing it to escape, think twice. Jacqueline, age 32, explains: "After breaking up with Andrew, I moved as far away from him as possible—to the opposite coast. Seattle was very fashionable at the time, and I thought it would be a good place to start over. I'd made such a mess of things in New York, and it was so full of memories and people Andrew and I knew in common, I just wanted to go somewhere I didn't know anyone."

But, for Jacqueline, Seattle's grunge-bar glamour and coffee-shop hipness wasn't enough. Separating herself from her support system and stable environment during her time of need only added to her misery. "I was very lonely. It was a mistake to rearrange my life because of something that someone else did. Andrew cheated on me—he was the one who had done something wrong. I should have staked out my territory and told him 'This is my town, not yours.' Besides, none of my wardrobe worked out there. I didn't like flannel, and all my clothes were black. No one wears black in Seattle!"

Finally, Jacqueline returned to the life she had abandoned just to get away from Andrew. "Even though I had originally thought I was going out to Seattle to stay, I came back to New York after only ten months. It was thrilling moving back. By that time, I had realized that New York was my home, and everything I'd worked so hard to achieve before was still there—work, friendships, interests. I just needed to be on my own instead of with butthead Andrew."

If you can't move—or don't want to—you may want to try rearranging your apartment. Buy satin sheets. Put up new pictures. Move the furniture around (especially your bed). You're leading a new life now. Why not make your surroundings reflect that?

Ten More Ways to Take Charge of Your Life

1. Make a list of your positive attributes. What are your strengths? What do you have to offer—not just to a boyfriend, but to the world? It's easy to get down on yourself after a breakup, but this exercise should help you see that you are a good person after all.

2. Don't feel compelled to go to bars, clubs, or parties just because everyone is encouraging you to go out and meet a new man now. Instead, do things that interest you. Even if you never meet a soul in your sculpting course, you'll still learn how to sculpt. But if you're going somewhere with the sole purpose of meeting someone and no one asks for your number, you'll feel like a failure. Besides, you should be worrying about yourself right now, not your future boyfriend. Dating again will come later (specifically, in chapter 7).

3. Improve your self-confidence by visualizing yourself happy without your ex. To get

started, try picturing yourself talking to people at a party. Imagine their reactions to your witty conversation and charming demeanor. Visualize them falling all over themselves to get you another drink. See them on their way home daydreaming about what their lives would be like if they were as cool as you. Whatever it takes!

4. Do something creative with your hands by joining a ceramics, glass-making, or woodworking class. "This is very therapeautic because it breaks the negative state you're in," says Childs. "One of the best ways to overcome your feelings of loss is to create something new."

5. Reach out to someone. When you feel worthless and unwanted, nothing lifts you up like helping somebody else. Do something for a loved one, or volunteer at a nursing home. Devote the time you're tempted to spend making him a special card or a knitted scarf to making them for a friend or someone in need instead. They'll be sure to appreciate it more.

6. Over time, revisit all the places you and your ex used to go together with good friends instead. The first time you go back, do something special: Order the most expensive thing on the menu at the restaurant you both used to love, flirt shamelessly with the bartender at the pub around the corner from his apartment, have a three-hour picnic in the park where you used to play Frisbee on Sunday afternoons. To help you replace the bad as-

sociations you have for these places with good ones, consciously do new things there that you know you'll remember. Eventually, going there won't seem painful at all.

7. Pamper yourself. Add up all the money you would have spent on him this year on gifts for his birthday, your anniversary, Valentine's Day, and the holidays. Then think up creative ways to spend it on yourself instead! Hire a cleaning service once a month. Buy a ridiculously overpriced new outfit. Spend a weekend at a posh spa.

8. Think about what you'd do for a friend going through a breakup, and do that for yourself. Make sure you're taking care of you. Treat yourself to an ice-cream cone, a new book, a day at the beach.

9. Consider what you might be missing besides your ex. What else was going on while you were dating him? Did you have a great job? Was it your first time on your own? Did you live with him in a cozy apartment in a nice area of town? You may be associating whatever good was in your life at that time with the relationship—but some of what you were enjoying had nothing to do with your ex. Can you recreate some of the other aspects of those good old days?

10. Learn to like being by yourself. "If you feel lonely, it could go back to a fear of abandonment from childhood," says Dr. Peterson. But you're an adult now, and you can get along on your own. "Take a bubble bath or go to the movies alone," advises Dr. Peterson. "It

feels weird at first, but you can learn to enjoy solitude. If your loneliness doesn't subside after a few months, it's a good idea to see a therapist."

But you may turn out just fine. Says Lana, age 23: "It was hard at first, but in the end I had a great summer. I was doing an internship in an art gallery, going to the beach, and spending a lot of time with friends and family. I decided it was an exciting time in my life, and there were other men out there who would appreciate me. All my friends were around, and they were supportive and kept me busy. I realized my life could be fun without him in it."

The Big Talk

Now that you've spent some time concentrating on yourself, you're starting to feel stronger. You're no longer going through thirty-seven boxes of tissues a day. You've had time to think about what went wrong and have begun to work through your pain. But before you can fully shut (or slam) the door on your old relationship, you need to get complete closure. And the best way to do that is to talk to your ex.

Talk to your ex? If the mere thought makes you nervous, it's not surprising. But now that you've gotten some distance from the situation, a lot of good can come out of meeting up with your old flame. It can give you perspective on the relationship that you might not otherwise gain. It can help you deal with any guilt you're experiencing over unresolved issues. And it will give both of you an invaluable opportunity to apologize for anything you may now regret. As Peter Sheras, Ph.D., a clinical psychologist at the University of Virginia, puts it, "It's good to go back to forgive—and be forgiven."

Who knows? It may even lay the groundwork for a beautiful friendship.

Are You Ready?

Wait until at least a few months after the breakup to call him. That way, you'll have had time to grow apart from him and move on with life on your own. Don't rush yourself. If you're secretly hoping that meeting up again will pave the way for a reconciliation, put that phone back down. You must accept the breakup before you see him again; otherwise, you'll just end up trying to talk him into getting back together.

"Be honest with yourself," says Dr. Mojas. "Here's a test: Could you handle hanging out with him and a new girlfriend? The answer will probably tell you whether or not you're ready to see him." Some people take longer than others to deal with the pain of a breakup. No matter how long ago you split up, it's never too late to talk to him. No, he hasn't forgotten who you are, and believe it or not, he might actually like hearing from you.

Let's Do Lunch

Forget about having a heart-to-heart over telephone lines. You want the sort of honest, meaningful conversation better facilitated by a face-to-face chat. So ask your ex to lunch: Since meeting for a midday meal is brief, casual, and public, it's perfect for the occasion. But don't suggest the restaurant you both used to love. Instead, choose one of your favorite new spots to reflect your new liberated life.

Now all you have to do is call him to make the plans. So gather your wits, practice sounding upbeat, and dial his number. Start off with something like "Listen, I know it's been a while, but I'd really like to get together as friends for lunch sometime soon. How's next week for you?"

If he says he's too busy right now, just say, "Okay, well, why don't you call me when you're free?" If you still haven't heard from him after another couple of weeks, call him again to remind him. If he refuses to get together with you at all, accept it. Simply say "Well, I'm sorry to hear you feel that way. If you change your mind, please give me a call."

But most likely, he'll agree. After all, you used to be a major part of his life; it's only natural that he'd be curious about what you're doing now. Still, even if he seems receptive, don't stay on the phone too long. Heavy conversation should be saved for when you see him. As soon as you've set your date, announce "Great! I'm looking forward to it," and say good-bye.

If you start to feel uneasy as the day of your lunch approaches, pretend you're just going to see an old friend. Remember, your ex is only as important to you as you let him be. As you get ready, keep a few things in mind. You'll want to look good, of course—but not too good. Don't send mixed signals by getting all dolled up. Keep your makeup fresh and natural. And leave the brand-new outfit (or the old one he always said he loved you in) hanging in your closet—choose something comfortable and understated instead.

Leave yourself extra time to get to the restaurant; that way, you can compose yourself beforehand, just as you might prior to an important job interview. If you feel your heart speed up for a sec when you first catch a glimpse of your ex walking in the door, don't worry about it. After all, you thought he was attractive when you were dating him. Why would you think any differently now? Besides, your accelerating heartbeat could just be a case of nervous jitters. Take a deep breath—you'll be fine.

If you're dating someone new, don't keep your lunch with your ex a secret. Instead, be honest with your boyfriend. You can reduce his anxiety about the situation by telling him what you're trying to accomplish and scheduling drinks with him straight after work that day. That way, you'll reassure him that your intentions are to get closure, not reignite sparks with your old flame.

What to Talk About

Greet your ex with a hug or a hand on his shoulder, if it feels right. Otherwise, just smile warmly, say hi and sit down. Tell him it's good to see him again. Be friendly, not aloof; remember, you want him to open up to you.

If you're afraid you might lose control of your emotions, pretend someone you really respect—

maybe a good friend or even a parent—is sitting at the table with you, listening in. Then promise yourself you won't do anything you wouldn't want them to know about. That should help you keep the conversation focused and mature.

Start things off by asking him about his family, friends, work—whatever you're genuinely interested in. Ask how he's been for the past few months. Tell him what you've been up to. If you've got a new boyfriend, go ahead and mention it, but spare him the details. Instead of trying to impress him, just be cheerful and honest.

Then move on to the bigger issue: why your relationship didn't work out. "Some men won't be responsive to this," warns Hillyer, "but others will sit down and be honest with you. It's important to keep your mind open to what he has to say, even if it's painful." Don't put him on the defensive with a comment such as "You weren't very supportive of me while we were together, were you?" At the same time, don't sell yourself short. A remark like "I guess things didn't work out because I was too selfish, huh?" does no one any good. Approaching the topic with an open-ended question will maximize your chances of getting the most out of the discussion. Simply say something like "What happened with us, anyway?" Even if you think you already know, it can be tremendously helpful to get his take on the situation.

You may discover it really was your *differences*, not you, that pushed you apart. Lance, age 25: "Cheryl and I broke up because my friend Lissa was having a party at my place. Her apartment was too small, so I told her I'd do her the favor.

But when Cheryl found out, she was upset that I hadn't asked her permission first. See, Lissa is best friends with Rachel, one of my ex-girlfriends, so of course Rachel would be at the party." And since, years earlier, Lance had once dumped Cheryl for a reconciliation with Rachel, Cheryl hated her. "She refused to meet Rachel, and she hated anybody who was friends with her. But Lissa was a very good friend of mine, and she was in a crunch, so I decided to have the party anyway. Cheryl and I ended up having a screaming match and eventually breaking up over it."

Melrose Place–style melodramas notwithstanding, Lance and Cheryl eventually did try to talk things over. "Months later, we met for coffee, and she wanted me to apologize. I apologized for upsetting her, but I don't believe I made a mistake about having the party. In her mind, it's my fault we broke up—she broke it off because I screwed up. But in my mind, it ended because we are two very different people. She was probably one of the smartest, nicest, most beautiful girls I ever dated, but we don't think the same way in terms of values and what's right and what's wrong. I could have saved the relationship by giving up my pride and my morals, but no one is worth that."

So take turns talking about what hurt you, what you did wrong, what you learned, what you miss. The meeting could even offer the chance for you both to admit how much you cared, even though the relationship didn't last. And if the breakup gave your self-esteem a beating, hearing that it really wasn't all your fault can be quite a comfort.

"When one of my exes broke up with me, it was incredibly painful for a really long time," explains Ivy, age 27. "But six months later, I felt I was ready to see him. I had gotten away from him for half a year, cut off all ties, and the whole healing process had kicked in. I felt really good, so I called him and asked him to meet me the following Sunday afternoon.

"We started out by discussing some friends I hadn't seen since the breakup. He said, 'So-and-so thought I was crazy for breaking up with you,' and 'You're so beautiful; everyone thinks you're beautiful, Ivy.' He never said such complimentary things when we were in a relationship, so they were good to hear.

"We eased into the conversation gradually. I guess at first he felt more comfortable talking about where he was at in his life rather than his feelings about us. But after we caught up, we talked quite a bit about our relationship. He'd say things like 'Do you remember this or that?' and I'd be like, 'Yeah, we were really stupid about that' or 'I know, I can't believe I was so bossy.' It was great for both of us to say 'I really learned from that—I'm not going to do that again,' out loud. We could've said things to hurt each other's feelings, but we kept it constructive."

All in all, Ivy advocates talking things over with your ex to help you both feel better. "I've had talks like this with several ex-boyfriends in the past and have never regretted it, no matter which side of the fence I was on. You're acknowledging that the relationship didn't work out, but you still care about each other and like each other enough to meet and discuss it. It's good to wait a bit before meeting up. After a while, you forget a lot of the bad stuff and just recall how much fun it was being with him. You remember the lightness of your relationship instead of the heaviness."

What If He Upsets Me?

If you both have the right attitude, your talk can be a great opportunity for healing. However, be prepared: Your ex could end up saying things that hurt you instead. If he tells you something like "You were terrible in bed" or "I never loved you," stay calm and consider the source. How much would you trust his opinion on other matters? "Ask him 'Why was that a secret you never shared with me?'" advises Dr. Lutwin. "Get a definite answer. Is he just preserving his male ego? Why is he telling you this now?"

Yes, his words still sting. But if these things were true, why would he have stayed with you as long as he did? He may just be trying to hurt you now because he's jealous of the fact that you're doing well and moving on. Or maybe he's on a power trip and wants to prove to himself that he can still get to you.

You might even become upset about what he doesn't say. "I saw Jason once before I moved away," says Julie, age 25. "I told him, 'You were my first love, and I'll always care about what happens to you. You'll always be important to me.' I hoped to get some sort of closure. I wanted him to say the things he would never even say during our relationship, to tell me I was important to him, too. Instead, he just said, 'Thanks.' That was it. Although I knew I shouldn't care what he thought, it still hurt."

If you start to cry, either because you're feeling hurt or you're missing the good old days, excuse yourself and head for the ladies' to compose yourself. If you become so upset that you don't think you can make it through the meal, get up and leave. Simply say "I'm sorry. I have to go." If you want to try again another time, tell him you'll call him. Later, ask a good friend if you could set up a dress rehearsal with her so you'll be less likely to lose your cool next time.

Whether or not you want to set up another meeting with your ex, it can be helpful to confide in a friend about what happened. You may also want to write down what the meeting was like in your postbreakup notebook. But don't beat yourself up. Even if you think some of his criticism was right on, remember that your relationship is over now, and though you can't change the past, you can learn from it to make a better future.

What If He's Too Far Away?

If you can't set up a meeting in person because it was a long-distance romance or one of you moved, you'll have to call or write instead. Talking on the phone gives you the opportunity to directly respond to what he's saying—and vice versa. However, it also means you might not be able to say everything you want to say. If he feels uncomfortable with the conversation, it's easy for him to cut it short: Suddenly he's on his way out the door, or he thinks he hears call waiting beeping in. (Yeah, right.)

That's why Marcie, age 25, wrote a letter to her ex. After a whirlwind three-week romance while abroad for a summer, she had to return to the States, putting an ocean between her and David, the man she'd fallen in love with. And since things hadn't gone smoothly right before her departure, leaving was doubly difficult. "A few days before I had to leave, he wasn't paying much attention to me, so I got really angry and told him he shouldn't treat me like that. Then he started holding my hand and being really nice to me again. But the night before I left, he got mad that I was hanging out with friends instead of waiting for him when he got off work. The next morning, he didn't even say good-bye. He just ignored me."

Once back in the States, Marcie felt very confused. "I wrote him a letter—not to win him back, but to find out where he stood. I still thought of him after six months and wondered if he thought of me at all." But David never wrote back. "He had a big ego, so he always had a hard time apologizing. I just wanted it to end officially; I think that's what bothered me the most. But then I realized I wanted someone who expressed his feelings and communicated more than David had."

Although sending him a letter does allow you to tell him everything you want to say, it also has one big drawback: You can't guarantee a reply, as Marcie's story illustrates. However, you may find that just writing the letter gives you the catharsis you need.

Reinventing Yourself

What If He Won't Meet?

If your ex refuses to talk to you, you'll have to give yourself your own closure. Ditto if the guy was abusive—subjecting yourself to the possibility of more abuse (whether mental or physical) isn't healthy. How do you get the closure you need? Ask a friend to meet with you instead. Tell her you want her to help you put this relationship to eternal rest once and for all.

Meet her where you'd have gone with your ex, and calmly go over everything you would have liked to have been able to talk to him about. For example, you might say "It really upset me when he put me down all the time; I didn't deserve that kind of treatment" or "I'm sorry I got so jealous whenever his ex-girlfriend called; I knew they were just friends, and I should have accepted that."

Your friend doesn't have to do anything but listen, nod her head occasionally, and offer a few affirming words. But somehow when you just say these lingering thoughts out loud, it can really clear your mind. Get out all the things you want to say, then buy your friend a celebratory drink.

Can't We All Just Get Along?

Suppose your lunch is ending, your talk went well, and you'd now like to establish a friendship with your ex. If that's the case, finish up your discussion by saying, "Why don't you give me a call sometime? I think it'd be fun to hang out as friends." That way, you let him know what you want, but don't force the issue by trying to make specific plans.

But before you ask him, ask yourself: Can you really be pals? Now that you've had some serious time apart, you may think you're ready for friendship. But think twice. Maybe you like the idea of being buddies. But after your talk, you find you're still in love with him, or you still want to sleep with him, or you still feel vindictive toward him. If that's the case, forget it. A friendship built on hidden agendas is no friendship at all.

"I was trying to be a good person and be friends with Justin," says Kristen, age 22, "but we just got into fights all the time. He would blow me off and not return my calls. I often found excuses to go over to his dorm room to borrow a tape or to see if he wanted to grab lunch in the cafeteria. This was all done under a friendly pretense, but I had ulterior motives. I would invite him to do stuff we had shared in the past, hoping maybe he would remember our good times. But little by little I realized I couldn't have a good relationship with someone who kept pushing me away."

If your ex doesn't want to be friends, don't take it personally: Maybe he can tell you're not ready. Maybe he's dating someone new who can't handle his being in contact with you. Or maybe he can't handle it. Some people find it too difficult to maintain friendships with old lovers. And no question, it is hard.

Dawn, age 30, should know. "Robert and I had this whole let's-be-buddies lunch recently, and I said something like 'Too bad we met at the wrong time.'" But Robert disagreed. "He thought there were other problems. We always used to have these heated discussions about random topics—like why women are obsessed with shoes and men aren't, for example. Robert fancies himself an intellectual and likes to play devil's advocate, but that's not my style." In fact, over lunch, it seemed that all Robert wanted to do was bicker. "He kept criticizing me, saying I was too stressed-out and got too frustrated. It was too confrontational for me. I thought, 'Screw it, what am I going to get from a friendship with him?'"

On the other hand, your ex may be very open to the possibility of friendship. "I don't like a total break in contact," says Lance, age 25. "A total break means you never had a friend in the first place, that you were just having sex with somebody. I dated my ex because she had something to say to me and I had something to say to her. That hasn't changed."

If you're both willing to forgive and forget, a friendship is a real possibility, as Robin, age 24, and her ex prove. "I've known Aaron for seven years and dated him for five, so he is a very big part of my memories. When it comes down to it, I still think he's a very good person who handled a situation badly. I speak to him about once a month now, just to touch base and say hello. I think once I realized that he was not the man of my dreams, I was pretty cool with the whole thing. I'm not going to marry him, so who cares? As flippant as that sounds, it's true."

Although it's tough, you might even become very close again—but this time as friends rather than lovers. Says Lori, age 24, "I met Sam while traveling in Israel six years ago. We hit it off, and after I left, we wrote to each other for two years. When I returned to Israel to go to school there for a summer, we immediately started dating. The day I arrived in Jerusalem, we got together.

"But the relationship ended two months later, when I had to return home to finish my studies. Had he come right out and said he didn't want me to leave, I probably would have tried a lot harder to stay in Israel. But he never did. On the plane going home, I was sobbing incessantly. The only reason we broke up was that I had to leave the country—it wasn't because we hated each other or anything like that. I think that made it all the more difficult to get on with my life, because I already knew the perfect guy was out there. He just wasn't here.

"It took me two years to stop pining after him, though I thought I was fine after one. I started going out with someone else, but at the first sign of trouble I would start thinking about my ex. That's when I realized I still wasn't over him. I figured the only way to stop obsessing was to go back to Israel and see him.

"So I went back two years ago. My excuse was that my best friend had just moved there, but part of my mission was to talk to Sam. I stayed with him, which was great, except for the night his new girlfriend slept over and I started bawling my eyes out in my room, cursing myself for deciding to go back.

"But eventually I did confront Sam about my feelings, and we talked about our relationship. One night—when his girlfriend wasn't around, obviously—I told him I truly believe that if I hadn't left we would still be going out because we were still so close as friends. He said, 'Yeah, but you can't think that way anymore.' The way he said it and the look in his eyes made me realize I wasn't the only one screwed up for the last two years.

"Just seeing Sam again and talking to him helped me carry on with my life. He didn't tell me as much as I wanted to hear, but he said enough. And that was ninety percent of the recovery. I felt I was over him. I knew I still loved him, but I also knew I could have a life without him.

"Since that time, we've gotten to the point where I know I can call him whenever I want, and it will feel like we just spoke the day before. Although it's so expensive for us to talk, he sometimes calls me three times in the same week. In fact, I just spoke to him and his girlfriend yesterday; I'm going to go see him again in two weeks. I now consider him one of my closest friends."

7

Starting Over

Close your eyes for a moment. (Well, read this paragraph first, then close your eyes.) Imagine yourself on a date. Not with your ex, but with someone new. Someone gorgeous. Heck, Matthew McConaughey, all right? He came to pick you up, handed you a dozen roses, took you out for a candlelit dinner, and is now sitting next to you on your couch. Looking into your eyes, he brushes a strand of hair off your face and whispers, "You know, you're the most amazing woman I've ever met." Then he takes your hands in his. "I'm afraid I've fallen hopelessly in love with you."

Feels good, doesn't it? Well, it's good for you, too; dating again could be just what you need now. After all, whether your relationship with Matthew turns out to be permanent or not, seeing a new guy shows you there's more to life than just your ex. There are other men who will find you attractive. There are other men you'll enjoy being with. Eventually, there are even other men to fall in love with—and who will fall in love with you right back.

Still not convinced there's anyone out there who can match up to your ex? If you alter your expectations, you might be pleasantly surprised. As Dr. Peterson puts it, "You may fear your ex-boyfriend was your last chance for true love. You feel you will never love that strongly or deeply again. But that's not true. There are billions of people on this planet, so there's got to be someone else out there who can meet your needs, especially since your ex couldn't! Now you can say 'Not only do I want the good parts of the relationship I've left, but I deserve to have a relationship which also has the missing elements the old relationship didn't have.'"

So get back out there and date some guys! Here you'll get the scoop on how to get psyched for it and what to watch out for.

It's Raining Men

When you were in a relationship, every time you saw a good-looking guy, you had to ignore it. Your closest friend's cute cousin, the adorable waiter at the cafe down the street, the sexy guy who came to fix your roof... Every one of them used to be off-limits, but no longer. Now you can date all of them at once if you like. There's an amazing freedom in that—enjoy it!

If you still haven't quite gotten over your feelings of rejection from the breakup, dating lots of new guys will do wonders for your confidence, as Karrie, age 26, reports. "Not long after breaking up with Ryan, I started dating three guys at the same time. It was fun and exciting, and it made me feel better about myself. I thought, 'So that loser didn't want me. Who needs him?'" Only a month or two ago, as you'll recall, you were crying into your pillow every night, but not anymore. As Karrie puts it, "Suddenly I was juggling men, on the phone with one guy while another beeped in!"

Of course, it may take you longer than two or three weeks to feel ready to date again. Some people need a few months to heal before they can face going out with new guys. But if it's been longer than that, ask yourself why you're avoiding it. Are you afraid of getting hurt? Unfortunately, I can't dismiss that fear outright. Within three months of my breakup with James, I actually got stood up by two different men in one weekend! However, on the other hand, I've also had some wonderful dates with some really sweet guys that I would have missed out on had I refused to date anyone at all.

If it's another breakup you're scared of, you're getting too far ahead of yourself. Instead of feeling you have to turn every date into your next big relationship, try to relax and just have fun. Right now you should be looking for men to join you for an enjoyable evening, not an entire lifetime.

Party Girl

Wondering how you'll meet said men? My favorite technique is to throw a wild party. It'll lift your spirits, help you reconnect with old friends you've lost touch with, and get you back into the social swing of things. After all, if you invite people to your soirees, they'll be more likely to invite you to theirs.

And as the hostess with the mostest, you enjoy all sorts of advantages on the man front (or is that man *hunt?*). For example, you can tell everyone to bring their friends—especially those of the male gender. Hey, as long as it's your shindig, you may as well maximize the number of hookup possibilities, right? Plus, thanks to the fact that you'll know most of the people there, you'll seem extra popular and in demand, which will both impress guys and make you feel more confident. And finally, since it is, after all, your party, you'll have an instant icebreaker to use on any good-looking guests you want to get to know: Introduce yourself, explain that it's your party, and say that you're trying to be a good hostess by greeting everyone. Ask who he came with, offer to get him a drink.

Best of all, having a party is the perfect no-pressure way to let brand-new (or long-standing) crushes know you're interested. For example, two months after James and I broke up, I went to someone else's roof party and met Warren, a guy I immediately hit it off with. However, since an annoyed neighbor in the next building was throwing buckets of water on us from her balcony, the party broke up before I got to talk to him for long. So as we walked down the stairs, I nonchalantly said, "Hey, I'm having a party soon. I have to talk to my roommate before I know for sure when it's going to be, but if you give me your number, I'll call and invite you!" Warren gave me his card.

I decided to schedule the shindig for two weeks later. When I called Warren to officially extend the invitation, he asked me out to dinner the next weekend. The party ploy was working perfectly! We planned to meet at a downtown restaurant that I'd never been to before, and for once I was right on time.

As I walked in the door, I heard someone say my name, and when I looked up, there was Brent, a gorgeous bartender I'd met a year earlier at my old neighborhood hangout. From what I'd heard, he'd moved to California—but it turned out he'd just taken a trip, returned, and gotten a job somewhere else.

I exclaimed, "Welcome back!" and couldn't believe my luck. Because it was my first date since breaking up with James, I had spent an hour on my hair and makeup and was dressed to kill—and here in front of me appeared a guy I had swooned over since the day we met. (Only now I was available!) As Brent mixed me a complimentary cocktail, we caught up for a few minutes, and then, since Warren was tardy, I popped the question. "So, Brent," I said, "I'm throwing a party next week—want to come? Give me your number and I'll call you with details. . . ."

And sure enough, by the time my date arrived, I'd already gotten another guy's seven digits! Suddenly, my newfound freedom felt nothing short of fantastic. I had a great dinner with Warren and spoke to Brent a few days later.

Although I was disappointed to hear he had to work the night of my party, Brent asked me to a concert the following week. We had a fabulous time and ended up staying out until four in the morning.

While inviting someone to a party isn't exactly asking someone out, it is sending him a message that you're interested. And once guys feel confident that you'll be receptive, they'll often make a move of their own. Case in point: I invited four guys I had crushes on to that party, and I ended up dating three of them. Granted, none of them turned into major relationships, but that shouldn't be what you're looking for now anyway.

P.S. If you really want to guarantee turnout, give your party a theme. For example, a few months ago, I threw a prom party, complete with balloons, streamers, spiked punch, king and queen elections, and mix tapes of all the music that was popular the year I graduated from high school. Most female guests wore old prom gowns or bridesmaid's dresses, while a lot of guys came in suits or tuxes. The novelty encouraged lots of mingling and conversation—and I met yet another date!

Here are a few more man-meeting tips to try:

- **Volunteer**. Are you concerned about environmental issues? Would you like to get involved with a political campaign? Do you want to help out at your local theater or homeless shelter? There is an organization that would love to hear from you. And since anyone you'll meet while volunteering is sure to share a common interest and likely to have a caring nature, it should be easy to strike up a conversation.

- **Join a club.** Whatever you're into, there's probably a group for you. For example, if you enjoy sipping chardonnay, you might want to try Wine B.R.A.T.S., a wine-appreciation organization for men and women ages 21 to 36 (call 1-707-545-4699 to find out about a chapter near you). Or try a ski club—weekend trips to the mountains should give you ample opportunity to mingle with members on the bus, on the slopes, and over hot chocolates back at the lodge.

  If you like biking, head for a bicycle shop and check their bulletin boards for flyers advertising local bike clubs. Join a professional organization, or sign up with a local coed choir or sports team. For more ideas, look through the listings in your local paper's weekend section. Or start your own club. Just think: You can have fun *and* meet a man, all in one fell swoop!

- **Get smart.** Continuing-education classes are educational (obviously), enjoyable, and a great place to meet guys. Hint: For the optimal male-female ratio, skip the sewing seminars and take Mechanics 101 instead.

- **Join a health club.** Yes, you'll be sweaty and barely clothed. But so will the guy on the neighboring Nautilus. So go ahead, check him out, say hi, and ask for advice on the proper exercise to strengthen your inner thighs.

- **Be a klutz.** Go ice-skating and "accidentally" bump into that hot guy gliding around the rink, then claim it was an accident. Tell him you've been trying to learn how to stop, but you can't quite get the hang of it. Could he help you out?

- **Ask your friends to set you up.** "Oh, no," you say. "Please, I've already been through a breakup. Now you want me to go on a blind date? Have mercy!" Yeah, yeah. But the truth is, blind dates get a bad rap. After all, since your personal Cupid knows you *and* the guy, the chance of sparks (and possibly even full-fledged fireworks) is a lot greater than if you're meeting some random cute guy in a club.

  Melissa, age 33, can vouch for that. "Two months after I broke up with Luke, my boss set me up on a blind date. On the way there, I thought, 'This is so stupid. I'm not over Luke. Why am I going?' But when I met Frank at the restaurant, he surprised me. It took a half hour or so, but we clicked. By the end of the dinner, we were holding hands. We stayed out until two in the morning, and the next day he left me a message on my voice mail. It just felt right, so I decided to go with it. In fact, we just got married!"

  Blind dates are like the lottery—hey, you never know!—except blind dates offer far better odds. So don't be shy. Treat finding a new man like finding a new job: Start networking! Tell everyone you know that you're available again, let them know you're interested in dating, and ask them if they have any cute single friends.

  You might even want to write a mock personal ad (or a real one—see below) in the notebook you've kept since your breakup. That can help you provide friends with some guidelines on what you're looking for. Are you after an educated, religious, career-oriented, Republican vegetarian? Of course, you should keep an open mind; a great guy might not meet every single one of your prereqs, but you wouldn't want to miss meeting him because of it. However, that shouldn't be a problem if you explain to friends that your guidelines are just that—guidelines—and aren't set in stone.

You should also reassure your friends that you won't hold it against them if their setup crashes and burns. Just as people call you about jobs that aren't quite right for you when they hear you're looking for work, so will they fix you up with men you won't quite click with when they hear you're looking for a new guy. That doesn't mean you don't want to hear about any new job openings, just as it doesn't mean you won't consider another blind date. So take the pressure off the matchmaker, and your friends will be a lot more likely to help you out.

- **Place a personal ad**. Advertising in a local paper is a great way to meet available men and boost your self-esteem. What girl coming off a breakup wouldn't want to hear from dozens of guys clamoring to go out with her? You're broadening your horizons and allowing yourself to test the waters again. Plus, by specifying what you want in your personal ad, you're declaring that you are in control of your love life and that guys who don't meet your criteria need not apply.

"I put in a personal ad because I was sick of the bar scene and ready for a committed relationship," says Lizzie, age 31. "I was tired of leaving things up to chance. I decided I needed to take action, and that's just what I did. I got tons of reponses, and I felt fabulous.

"Right away, I was closer to getting what I wanted in a guy. Everyone who answered was in the right age group, had a college education and a good job, and was a nonsmoker—just what I'd asked for. I met this awesome guy I never would have met otherwise. He's in finance and I'm in publishing, so we don't hang out in the same circles. But he was exactly the kind of quality person I'd been looking for. And now we've been together seven months!"

The Art of the Pickup

Say you're at a bar or party. You're surrounded by stunning single men, yet at a loss as to how to meet any of them. So you stick close to your friends all night. Or you spend half the night in the bathroom, making sure your false eyelashes are on straight. Or you lean against a wall seductively, praying someone cute will come up and talk to you.

Although it would be nice if that's all you had to do, you'll find that actually making an effort vastly improves your odds. For starters, force yourself to talk to a good-looking guy. Say "Crazy weather we're having, huh?" or "How do you know the host?" But keep the small talk to a minimum. Think of how many times you've been asked: 1) What do you do? 2) Where do you live? 3) Where are you from? and 4) Where did you go to school? Although it's always nice to talk about yourself, you've probably answered these questions so many times now even you're a little bored with the answers.

Chances are, he feels the same way. So after a few pleasantries, direct the discussion down a more interesting path. Ask him a few offbeat questions, like "What was your favorite game as a child?", "What was the worst job you ever had?", or "Have you ever had an experience where you almost died?" You're still asking him about himself, but the conversation is suddenly a lot more stimulating. Making conversation other than the standard-issue small talk will set you apart as quirky, spontaneous, fun, unpredictable. I sometimes inquire, "What are your feelings about tanning?" It almost always gets an amused smile and a reply that starts with something like "Hmm, that's an interesting question...." From there, you can talk about the last time each of you went to the beach, whether he prefers the coast or the country, and so on.

By approaching him, you've put yourself in the driver's seat. Are you interested in what he has to say? If not, it's easy to excuse yourself; just say "Well, it was nice chatting with you, but I've got to go find my friends/refresh my drink/get in the bathroom line before it snakes out the front door." If, on the other hand, you find he's got the personality to go with the good looks, you can ask for his number. Say "Listen, it's been great talking to you, but I've got to go [fill in excuse from above]. In case I don't see you later, maybe I could get your number and we could get together some other time?" By being the one to end the conversation, you'll show him you're a girl with places to go and people to see. And if you get his number, you won't have to worry about waiting for him to ask for yours.

What if he says no? Well, he might. But if he does, at least you haven't wasted any more time on a guy who is taken, isn't interested, or can't handle an assertive woman. Hold your head high and move on to a guy who *is* worth your time.

Another idea: If it's a big, casual bar or party, bring along a bag of chips or cookies. I discovered this trick a few years ago: I hadn't had time to have dinner before I was supposed to meet a friend at a bar, so I grabbed a box of crackers at a store on the way. When I got to the bar and opened the box, I was suddenly the most popular girl there! When people drink, they get hungry—and you have food. If you simply stand there with it, guys will come to you.

You could also try looking—really looking—at men you're admiring from afar. When you catch their eye, hold your gaze for another full two seconds and smile slightly, then look away. This is very difficult. You will be tempted to avert your eyes as soon as he notices you're staring at him. But if you can keep up your gaze, you tell him two things: You're daring, which is incredibly sexy, and you're interested, which is incredibly encouraging.

If you do try this technique, wait for him to come to you. He'll probably continue to glance over several times to see if you're still looking at him; don't stare at him all night, but do let him "catch" you looking his way a few times. It's not unusual for a man to cross a room to talk to someone he sees doing this.

Want things to move a little faster? Follow 25-

year-old Jenni's lead. "I give a cute guy the look to show him I'm interested, then wait for him to look back. I repeat that move a couple of times, then 'happen' to have some sort of catastrophe in his general vicinity. 'Operation Earring' is my favorite. I walk over kind of to the side of him, so he can still see me, but not right in his face, where it would be too obvious. Then I get my hair caught in my hoop earring and try to look like I'm really struggling with it. Obviously he wants to come to my rescue, so he walks over to help me. Works every time, I swear. I've hooked up with a ton of guys this way."

Got short locks or unpierced ears? Get a drink and hold the change in your hand, then "drop" a few coins or a dollar as you walk by him; at a party, do this with a cocktail napkin instead. If you're feeling especially gutsy, wink at him (but only once—more is overkill) or even motion for him to come over. Try a few different techniques to see what works best for you.

One last tip: Grab a friend, stand near the guy you're interested in, and audibly argue about something—how to hold a golf club, for example, or what movie won the Oscar for Best Picture last year. You can even make a bet about it if you like. Then, after you've gone back and forth several times, lean over and ask him to settle your argument. And don't let it end there. Ask how he knows so much about golf. Or what film he thought *should* have won. Guess what? You're now in a conversation with him.

You've Got Some Nerves

So you've got a date—congratulations! Now all you have to do is relax. If the idea of going out with a new guy is freaking you out, remember, it doesn't have to be that way. Some things to keep in mind:

- Fake it till you make it. It's natural to feel anxious about seeing someone new. But if you act confident, you'll seem confident—and eventually, even *be* confident.
- Talk to yourself in the mirror before you go out. You'll feel silly, but it really does work! Say something like "I'm a sexy, wonderful woman, and tons of guys would count themselves lucky to date me." Then pull out a photo of yourself—alone or with friends, not your ex—where you know you look good. Before you leave, take a few minutes to study the snapshot and go over your personal assets list (see page 188). See? You *are* sexy and wonderful!
- Instead of thinking "I hope he likes me," think "I hope I like him!" That will help you focus on his behavior instead of worrying about your own.
- Practice breathing, speaking, and walking more slowly. See how much more calm and in control you feel? Next time you get nervous around a man, simply focus on slowing yourself down; it can make a big difference.
- Instead of dinner, have lunch on a first date; if you know it will only last an hour or so, it'll take a lot of the pressure off. Or, if you do get

together for coffee or drinks in the evening, schedule plans for later that night. That way, if it turns out you didn't like him as much as you thought you would, you have a convenient exit. On the other hand, if it turns out you really like him, being the first to say good night will increase his interest.

Beware of Instant Sex

So you've mastered meeting men and have even gone out with a few. Now what? If your first impulse is to try a little sexual healing, think twice.

You might imagine making a little sheet music would be just the thing to help you feel desirable again, but according to Dr. Peterson, "getting sexually involved right away is a mistake. Hopping into bed with someone isn't going to make you feel better. You don't need sex, you need affection—and confusing sex with intimacy is very dangerous in the age of AIDS. When you're feeling sad about your ex, you may do self-destructive things, like have what I call suicidal sex—unprotected sex with someone you don't know. Instead, take care of your sexual needs yourself."

Hillyer agrees. "You're better off not having a few sexual flings. The problem is that when women get sexually involved, we have a hard time not getting emotionally involved. And then it's too easy to start thinking relationship stuff when there still hasn't been real healing from the last one.

"If you do choose the fling route, you need to be careful, both physically and emotionally," continues Hillyer. "Don't get into any fantasies about what's happening if you know it's just fun and games and nothing else."

Lana, age 23, thought she could cope, but it turned out to be more difficult than she had anticipated. "I dated one younger guy I initially wanted only sex from," she remembers. "But I found it difficult to sleep with someone and then distance myself from him. In fact, when I found out he also only wanted to sleep with me, I was really hurt."

Right now you're still very vulnerable, and sex—recreational or otherwise—stirs up a lot of emotions. Are you sure you can manage that at the moment? Sure, it feels good while it lasts, but consider how you'll feel in the morning. "Sex is something you should do only when you're comfortable and ready," says Dr. Sheras. "For now, you're better off going out and having a good, stiff drink or renting a video."

Are You Shutting Men Out?

While it's not wise to get involved with every guy who comes along, it's also important not to close yourself off to the possibility of ever falling in love again. Says Hillyer, "When we get hurt from a breakup, we often protect ourselves by becoming bitter and resentful toward men. We get attracted to men who live in other cities or start feeling that none of them are good enough. If we do get into another relationship, we don't open up. But if you don't allow yourself to be vulnerable or trust the other person, you really can't have a good relationship."

Brenda, age 27, is a classic example. "I'm afraid to date since I broke up with Eddie. I really haven't dated at all. I did get involved with my roommate, but he was moving to another state, so it only lasted a few weeks. We talked a lot and he knew all about my breakup. When things got romantic between us, I didn't sleep with him, but we kissed and fooled around, and it was really difficult for me. I felt like I was cheating on Eddie. Isn't that horrible?

"There is a guy at work—we have a lot of chemistry, and I feel like we've been seeing each other since I got my job. But he has a girlfriend. Now I'm looking for someone to marry, but I work a lot of hours, and the men I've met haven't been interesting enough to even try to date. But then I don't get to know them really, either, so...."

Look at all the "buts" in Brenda's story. Are you making similar excuses? Maybe you're having a lot of difficulty moving on. Lori, age 24, has been there. Although she couldn't stay in Israel, where she met her ex, she found it hard to leave Sam behind. "Sam called me right before my birthday, nearly a year after our breakup, and a new guy asked me out right afterward. I was so confused. I thought, 'Do I hang on to this guy in Israel, or do I start dating someone right here?' I went out with the new guy, but in retrospect, he never had a chance.

"We dated for about four months, but I thought about Sam a lot. The longer our relationship lasted, the more I compared the two of them, and obviously, the new guy lost. This was a definite sign that I was not over Sam, even though I thought I was."

If this sounds familiar, it's time to take a step back. Rejecting every guy who comes along or getting into brief relationships that never go anywhere isn't healthy. If it's been quite a while since your breakup and you still feel unable to get more than superficially involved with anyone else, you probably haven't come to terms with your loss.

Laura, age 25, certainly hasn't. "When I started dating a new guy, Keith, maybe a year after Pat and I broke up, I would always write lists of pros and cons comparing him to my ex. Keith would have almost no pros and tons of cons, and Pat would have no cons and tons of pros. My next serious boyfriend, Mike, took my mind off Pat somewhat, but I still always made comparisons. It's depressing because nothing can live up to my idea of what Pat and I had. He was my first love, and I just can't see much negative about our relationship.

"It's hard for me to find a guy I want to get serious with. My expectations are still based on my relationship with Pat. I'm not even sure I've stopped obsessing over him, and it's been five years since we broke up. I think about him every single day and can't seem to find anyone who measures up."

Keeping your distance protects you from being hurt, but it also keeps you hooked on your ex. Allowing yourself to get involved with someone else, on the other hand, can help you break free for good, even if things don't work out with someone new. "I started dating again seriously about nine months after Aaron and I broke up," says Robin, age 24. "I had been fixed up on dates prior to that, but hadn't given any of them much thought. It was kind of thrilling to date again, but I was really, really scared of getting hurt. In fact, I was so scared that I kind of blew it with the first great guy I met.

"But the next guy I dated was a great communicator who loved to talk about what he was thinking and how he was feeling. That just confirmed for me that my previous relationship was not meant to be. I had found this new courage that it was okay to go back out there, and I could stop clinging to the past."

And who knows? Things with you and your new boyfriend might work out just great. "After Jon broke up with me, I decided I was no longer going to pursue men or try to meet people," says Missy, age 27. "I dated people but wouldn't allow them to get close to me. I thought I just wasn't meant to be in a relationship. When I met Bruce, I was still very cynical. Bruce was the ultimate nice guy—too caring, too sensitive. He wasn't the type of person that I usually went for.

"But after dating him for a while, he made me realize that Jon had treated me miserably. I was so head over heels in love with Jon that I'd make excuses for him. When he'd tell me he'd call at a certain time, and then I didn't hear from him for days, I'd say, 'That's just Jon. He really does care, but that's just the way he is.' But Bruce always kept his word. With Bruce I would never worry that he would leave if I said or did the wrong thing, but with Jon I often felt that way. Bruce knew I had just gotten out of a relationship, and he was really patient and caring.

"In fact, on our third or fourth date, he said, 'Oh, I have something for you,' and then gave me a box of chocolates, all wrapped up. I thought it had to be a gift that he had been given by someone else. I seriously didn't believe for five full minutes that he had actually gone out and bought something just for me. I had never been with someone who would do that. Bruce showed me there are people out there who are loving, supportive, and sensitive." In fact, Missy and Bruce are now engaged.

Is He the Guy for You?

If you find a new man falling for you, it's tempting to go with the flow. After all, when you've been feeling lonely, what better cure than a new boyfriend? But your judgment may not be quite as sound as it should be at the moment, and if you jump into another relationship that isn't right for you, you'll just be guaranteeing yourself more pain down the road.

"Rushing into another relationship is the worst thing you can do—yet people do it all the time," says Childs. "No one likes feeling the loneliness that follows a breakup. People would rather just ease the pain with someone new. But that way, they don't ever get to learn about themselves. They lose the chance to heal and work through the grief."

According to Dr. Mojas, "Getting involved

with someone else immediately feels like a nice, quick fix. But if you haven't taken the time to learn from what happened in your old relationship, you're more likely to repeat the same mistakes or be blind to red flags about the new man in your life.

"For example, say the guy you broke up with had an alcohol problem. Maybe the new guy you get involved with doesn't drink, but you're completely overlooking the fact that he's a compulsive gambler. You're so excited this guy isn't an alcoholic that you give him a lot more credit than he deserves."

Says Julie, age 25, "Jason drank all the time, so when I met Paul, a sweet guy who was really into me, I was totally excited. But it turned out that he lied about everything, saying things like his band had a video on MTV and he was ranked third in the world in bodysurfing. I couldn't believe a thing he said! But I didn't dump him for months, mainly just because he wasn't wasted all the time."

Julie's story illustrates what can happen when you rush into a relationship too quickly. But say you've waited a while. You've thought about what you want. And you think the new guy you're seeing fits the bill. How do you know for sure? For starters, ask yourself a few key questions. If you weren't dating him, would you want to be friends with him? Is he honest? Caring? Trustworthy? Sensitive? Supportive? Think about what's important to you, and ask yourself if he measures up. You can use the same test on your new beau that you did on your ex: Does this guy have at least ninety percent of what you want from a man? (For details on this, flip back to page 61.)

Maybe you're worried that things don't seem as immediately intense with this guy as they did in your past relationships. But that's not necessarily a bad thing, as Hillyer explains. "Choosing someone who doesn't make you get all excited could be a healthy sign. The men we get gooey about tend to be our old type, our poison people. Subconsciously, we're drawn to men who echo old situations. If a parent was emotionally distant, you'll probably get gooey over emotionally unavailable men without even realizing it. There's an unconscious belief you'll get it right this time. The gooey feeling is often actually just an anxious reaction to that challenge."

After breaking up with an abusive ex, 25-year-old Jenni had to work hard to stop looking for that "gooey feeling," as she explains: "I started dating again pretty much right away, but I found I was choosing guys just like Brian, so I didn't get serious with anyone. I wasn't trusting at all. I became more leery of a guy who raised his voice or grabbed me like my ex did. Gradually, I started dumping the guys when I'd see the Brian signs. Now I'm dating a great guy who is totally not like that. We met through a personal ad. He is not the kind of person I ever would have given a chance to before I met Brian. But it's turned out to be the healthiest relationship I've ever been in."

Making Your New Relationship Work

Even when you find someone special, you may worry that it won't last. "The breakup has made me more cynical and jaded and gun-shy than ever," says Dawn, age 30. "I'd think, 'Why would this ever work out? It'll end in a fiery explosion just like everything else.' I'm dating a new guy now, and he's saying all these great things about me, but I feel I can't trust him. I can't even enjoy it. My ex said I was his best friend ever, I was the greatest, blah, blah, blah, but a couple of months later, he wasn't even talking to me."

If you've learned from your past mistakes, your new relationship can be different. But it won't happen automatically. Need help? Here are a few pointers:

- Ask him about his relationship history—and listen carefully. "Bringing it up on the third date is a safe bet," says Hillyer. "You don't want to scare him off by asking a lot of questions right off the bat. But on the other hand, you need answers fairly soon into the relationship. By then, you're past the initial getting-to-know-each-other stage, yet you still haven't invested too much time in your courtship."

Has he been married five times? Did he cheat on every girl he's ever dated? Is he rivaling Wilt Chamberlain for the title of Most Women Slept With? Don't think you'll be the one to change him. If he has had a lot of serious relationships end or has avoided getting serious at all in the past, what makes you think he'll act differently this time?

- Don't invest too much in the relationship too soon just because you're so happy to have a boyfriend again. Remember, you need to devote time and energy to yourself, not just your new relationship. Besides, being at his beck and call could come off as more smothering than sweet.

  And don't let yourself fall too fast. If he's charming and romantic and wonderful, great. But remember, in the beginning, you still don't really know him. Maybe he acts like this with every woman he dates. Let him earn your love. As Caitlin, age 25, puts it, "I was a little too open about personal stuff with some of the guys I dated after Billy. I am more guarded now. I don't believe in love at first sight anymore. I now know you have to go with something for a while and let it develop and grow. Sometimes it takes more time."

- Don't see every little problem as a sign your relationship won't work out. Instead, keep the lines of communication open, and deal with issues as they arise. If you get into a fight, rather than attacking him or getting defensive, pretend you're a third party trying to make peace.

  Suppose he always breaks plans. Instead of saying "I can't stand the way you never stick to your promises!", say "It often seems there's somewhere else you'd rather be than with me." Trying to understand where he's coming from by telling him how you're interpreting his words and actions will help you solve problems much more quickly and easily.

- Don't talk about your ex. Although you should be willing to discuss your relationship with your ex if asked, don't volunteer random information about him. Your new boyfriend doesn't want to know you still have sex dreams about your ex, he's not interested in the fact that he and your ex both go to sleep with their socks on, and he doesn't find it fascinating that, although he prefers Kool & the Gang's later albums, your ex favored their earlier work. The message here: Unless you are trying to make your new guy feel resentful, competitive, and irritated, quit bringing up your ex-boyfriend.
- Keep the relationship out of the bedroom for a while. After you go out with a new man a few times, he may start putting the moves on you. But if you don't feel ready, say so. "It's best not to go to bed with a new guy for three months, even if you think he is the man of your dreams," warns Childs. "You can't develop a friendship in less than that time, and he won't be able to maintain a persona for longer than that. Once you become bed partners, you'll go into denial; it's a defense mechanism.

"If you want someone who will listen to you and someone you can confide in, you have to check him out first. The first few weeks, he will say 'yes, yes, yes' and tell you what you want to hear. But by the end of three months, you'll have a pretty good idea of who that guy really is." If you feel you can't wait three whole months, wait as long as you can stand it. Hopping in the sack immediately may feel tempting, but it hurts your new relationship's chances in the long run. A man who can't handle holding off a little isn't worth your time; he obviously doesn't find you worth his. If you're feeling apprehensive about sleeping with someone new, waiting until you get to know and trust him will make you feel more comfortable—which, in turn, will make the sex between you even more fantastic.

Once you do decide to sleep together, don't bring your ex to bed with you: Don't fantasize about him, don't allow yourself to feel guilty about being with someone else, and don't compare your new boyfriend's technique with your ex's (especially not out loud!). Remember, you're with someone new now. If the sex isn't as electric as you'd hoped at first, give it time. It took you and your ex a while to learn the best ways to turn each other on; give this guy the same opportunity.

- Make sure you're judging your new boyfriend fairly. Are you always comparing him to your ex—and finding ways to make him fall short? Although you should certainly consider your priorities carefully, that doesn't mean a new guy should have to ace every last little test.

"My old boyfriend was a very sharp dresser—a real J. Crew type," says Karrie, 26. "After we broke up, this other totally hot guy asked me out, but he always wore his jeans tucked into his combat boots. At first I thought I could deal with it, but after a while, I found it embarrassing. We'd be walking down the street, and every time I looked down, all I could think was, 'Desert Storm is over! Untuck the pants!' "

Clearly, this is a crazy criterion, but if you haven't fully let go of your ex or the pain from the breakup, you may catch yourself making these sorts of comparisons yourself. If you do, it's wise to keep in mind that just because your new guy doesn't have one particular asset that your ex did, doesn't mean that his good points don't far outweigh your last boyfriend's. Demanding that the next man in your life be perfect is nothing more than a safe way to remain unattached.

Sign Language

Were you taken aback when your ex let you go? This time around, you don't have to be thrown for a loop. There are ways to know when a relationship's on the rocks, long before he utters a word about it. When love starts to go astray, he might not tell you directly—but if you can read the subtle signals, he won't have to. Any of these signs sound familiar?

He . . .

- Directs sarcastic remarks your way. ("Yeah, you're a *great* driver.")
- Loses interest in sex. ("Not tonight, honey. This migraine is kicking my butt.")
- Stops watching your favorite show with you every week. ("This story line is getting really stupid!")
- Complains about everyday stuff. ("I'm sick of your cat shedding all over my black coat.")

Starting Over

- Becomes very critical of you, even in front of others. ("You look like you've gained some weight.")
- Starts hanging out with more single guys, especially someone who has recently separated from his own girlfriend or wife. ("I can't see you tonight—I'm playing poker at Bob's.")
- Tries to change you. ("I wish you liked jazz/knew how to cook/wore fishnet stockings.")
- Takes time and energy from you and the relationship by throwing himself into work or spending more time with others. ("Looks like I'll be at the office until midnight at least.")
- Pursues new interests but doesn't include you. ("Fly-fishing with the boys is a blast!")
- Brings up more bad times than good in your relationship. ("Remember that huge fight we had at Niagara Falls last summer?")
- Has friends who act strange around you, like they know something you don't. (You: "Hi Bob! What's new?" Bob: "Uh . . . hi . . . um, excuse me—I have to go to the bathroom.")
- Starts to withdraw—watches more TV, works out for two hours, reads a lot. ("This new Tom Clancy novel is really a page-turner!")
- Stops sleeping in the same bed. ("Sorry I fell asleep on the couch again last night—I was really bushed.")
- Stops calling you by your pet name. (You: "Hey, snookums/muffin/chocolate-covered banana!" Him: "Hey.")
- Changes hairstyle or appearance. ("I'm going for a sort of Bruce Willis look.")

- Starts hanging out with a new group of friends. ("Those women from accounting really know how to tie one on!")
- Spends more time by himself. ("I just need some time on my own right now.")
- Criticizes your day-to-day lifestyle. ("Why do you always have to act like such an intellectual?")
- Tells you he'll never truly make you happy. ("You deserve better.")
- Says he can't commit. ("Marriage and me don't mix.")
- Fights with you over every little thing. ("How dare you say *The Brady Bunch* was better than *The Partridge Family!*")
- Doesn't return your calls. ("I never got the message—maybe something's wrong with my voice mail.")
- Makes excuses not to see you. ("Sorry, I really need to alphabetize my CD collection tonight.")
- Is "tired" on dates. ("My neighbor's pet rabbit has been keeping me up nights.")
- Distances himself from you when you're with a group. ("Uh, I think I'll sit over there by Jimmy—I haven't seen him in a while.")
- Avoids discussing the future or planning ahead. ("The Virgin Islands next month? Let me get back to you on that.")
- Never compliments you, even when you compliment him first. (You: "Honey, you look scrumptious tonight!" Him: "Thanks.")
- Is irritable or impatient with you. ("Can you pass me the bleepity-bleep crossword puzzle?")

Obviously, your relationship isn't automatically in trouble if your man sends just one of these signals. But if you're getting several of them repeatedly, it's time to take action. Although you may feel determined to change him, remember that nobody has the power to change another person. You only have power to change yourself. But that doesn't mean you have to sit back and take whatever he's dishing out. If you modify your own actions, he will almost certainly have to adjust his.

Acknowledging his behavior as soon as possible is key. Sure, it's easy to tell yourself, "Oh, it's no big deal" or just hope it will pass, but the earlier you bring it up, the better. If you try to understand and accept his inconsideration, you'll just encourage it, and you'll never be treated the way you deserve. Make it clear that you know your own self-worth and won't sacrifice your own happiness for his. If you value yourself, he'll be more likely to value you, too.

The first thing you need to do is to ask him what's going on. Childs suggests approaching him in a caring, nonjudgmental way. Say he's always dozing off in front of the TV these days, only coming to bed long after you're asleep. "You could say, 'I've noticed the past couple of weeks you've been really tired. I'm worried about you. Are you okay? Are you working too hard?' Present your questions in a curious manner that's not shaming. You need to demonstrate concern, love, and gentleness."

If you say, "I'm worried about your behavior—is anything wrong?" and he replies, "Nope, nothing," don't leave it at that. If he doesn't respond positively at first, give him two or three chances. Approach him in different ways. For example, you could first say you're concerned about him, mentioning a few troubling behaviors. If that doesn't work, wait a few days and mention that you've noticed that the two of you haven't been communicating in the relationship, and you're wondering if something has changed. If he still doesn't respond, give it a couple more days and say you're worried about the changes in your relationship and need his assurance that things are okay.

One more tip, courtesy of Dr. Cooper: "Avoid using 'you' messages such as 'You did this to me' or 'You always pull away.' You're only going to get a defensive response. Use an 'I' message instead, such as 'I feel hurt when I see you looking at other women' or 'I need more communication and affection.' If you're going to use the word 'you,' bury it at least five words into a sentence to avoid the judging message of a 'you' statement." That way, you're more likely to get a positive, honest reply.

But even if he does respond to your comments, the problem won't magically disappear. You've still got some work to do. Start by making a list of what you like and dislike about the relationship. "The two of you can write down what's been bothering you about each other," says Dr. Cooper. "This ensures that you've both heard each other out. Keep the list free of 'you' statements by writing in third person, such as 'He does this' or 'He doesn't do that.'"

Then write down what you *like* about the relationship and your mate. Usually the list of what you love about him will be far longer than the one of what you don't. "Fill up the positive list," advises Dr. Cooper, "so when he reads them both, he'll see the imbalance. That will show him that he's not the bad guy; instead, he's a good person who has some behaviors that don't work between the two of you. Hopefully, that will motivate him to communicate more."

"You should also grade the items on each list from one to ten," says Dr. Cooper. "That way, you'll both be able to see which items are really important to you and which are less so. "Being affectionate might rate an eight; cheating on you with your best friend is a ten," continues Dr. Cooper. "You may even want to add the numbers on each list to come up with two totals. You can use these to better communicate with your partner. When men are confronted with emotional issues they tend to respond by relying on logic, so using numbers can help."

After you've completed the lists, sit down and read them to each other. Tell him you need to have an understanding that he has heard and understood you, and vice versa. Discuss each point in detail. Cite specific examples without being accusatory. How are you going to improve matters? Are you both committed to the relationship? Making and discussing lists in this way can be a valuable tool when addressing unacceptable behavior and deciding whether to stick with the relationship or bail out. If you find that he's receptive to your concerns, but you continue to have problems, you may want to consider couples therapy.

However, if he never responded to your questions in the first place, or responded halfheartedly but then refused to even try making his lists, you have no choice but to do your own thing. Do you always want closeness while he always wants distance? Maybe you've been giving him far more attention than he needs; start pulling back. "Let him be the one who initiates the kiss and the hug," advises Dr. Cooper. "Then, when he does, reward him for his good behavior. It's like training a dog. Say, 'I love it when you touch me,' or rub his hand a little." Pursue your own interests and socialize with friends. Instead of waiting around for him, make plans with other people. Start rebuilding your support network and connecting with friends, so you won't be totally destroyed if this relationship doesn't work out. Do the things you've always wanted to do.

From End to Beginning

A few days after my ex-boyfriend broke up with me, I was sitting at my desk at work, unable to do anything but stare at my computer screen. I was supposed to be writing a magazine article, but instead I began typing out all the thoughts that were going through my mind. One passage seems particularly appropriate here: "Maybe later on, this hurt will somehow make me appreciate everything more. Is this building character?"

The answer, I know now, is yes. The beauty—and in a sense, the tragedy—of being an adult is that you can get over anything. And you're stronger, more independent, more compassionate as a result.

There is a certain joy, after all, in doing things for yourself. In the year and a half since James and I broke up, I've experienced many small moments of pleasure upon realizing that I could get along quite well in life without him. I'm no longer depending on someone else to make me happy—*I'm* making me happy.

And I can take care of myself just fine. One night while I was cutting a bagel, I sliced my finger right into the nail and had to walk to the emergency room alone, with layers of toilet paper wrapped around my finger. I was in pain but smiling a little nonetheless because I felt calm and confident that I could get through not only four stitches and a tetanus shot, but whatever life threw my way.

Many women have had similar experiences. "I grew up," says Lana, age 23. "I realized that I'm a terrific person and that people like me—not just men, but women, too. I had met Joshua my first day of classes, freshman year of college, and for four years I really didn't have any other friends. I've learned I don't need a boyfriend to be happy. A lot of my insecurities are gone, like low self-esteem and jealousy. I know I can be independent and satisfied on my own."

Thanks to the pain of your breakup, you too may have tapped into inner resources you weren't even aware you had. "Although I sometimes let myself get walked on in my relationship, I was strong enough not to let the breakup crush me," says Caitlin, age 25. "I was able to get up and move on." As Melissa, age 33, puts it, "My breakup was a defining moment for me. I'm a lot stronger than I thought I was. I will never be that vulnerable again."

The Finer Points of Freedom

It's okay to want another boyfriend in your future, but you shouldn't feel you *need* one to be happy. Don't get into a new relationship just because you don't want to be alone on a Saturday night. You need to experience getting along on your own and enjoying your own company. Then you can think about a relationship.

You may even find that, at this point in your life, you enjoy being unattached more than having a boyfriend. Mavis, age 20: "I always seem to get into serious relationships, even though I'm not looking for one. Right now, a relationship seems claustrophobic. I need to sow my wild oats."

On the other hand, if you want to get married and have kids someday, you may be getting nervous listening to your biological clock tick. But putting your love life on fast forward isn't the answer. After all, you want to be with a man because you're in love, not because you're in a hurry. Besides, taking your time doesn't automatically mean foregoing a family. "These days, many women are having babies later and later," notes Dr. Peterson. "I just had my first child at forty-one and a half!"

Instead of wishing you had a boyfriend, learn to be happy with your life the way it is. Says Dawn, age 30, "My friend Chris is thirty as well, and he's *reveling* in this whole bachelor guy thing.

He lives in a cabin, travels a lot, dates tons of women, and does whatever he wants. That makes me think, 'Why do I always have to worry about everything?' " Alter your attitude, and being single seems fabulous, not frightening.

You Deserve More

If your ex took you for granted, you may now realize you want more from a relationship. Says Dawn, "I'm never going to let someone treat me like that again. Finding the right relationship is still a big goal of mine, but the breakup has helped me focus on my need to be true to myself instead of getting pushed around."

Thinking about what happened between you and your ex can help you come to terms with what you want from a future relationship. How will things be different next time? What kind of relationship are you looking for? "I want someone who trusts me and who can be trusted one hundred thousand percent," says Kim, age 23. "I am the most important person in my life."

Kathy, age 24, also has a new outlook. "I'll never again try to convince someone that I'm important. My partner should know without my having to tell him. I've also decided I'm going to have a good time and not waste energy looking for the 'perfect' guy. If it happens, it happens."

Remember, even if your ex treated you well, you still broke up. I'm not going to pretend life is perfect for me now or that I don't still sometimes miss the times I had with James, but I'd rather be with someone who wants to share my life than someone who wasn't willing to stick around. I know I deserve better than that—and so do you.

Your Personal Growth Spurt

Obviously, when you break up with someone, your life changes drastically. But you may be surprised to find these changes are often for the better. "Eddie broke up with me so many times, but every breakup has catapulted me into the next stage of my life: going back to school, moving out of my parents' house, relocating to D.C., getting a job.... I needed to take on new challenges," says Brenda, age 27. "Eddie wasn't very supportive, so I think that's why I didn't do more when I was with him.

"Now I'm much stronger. I have a great job and live in a great city. I recently took up guitar and painting. I'm really just diving into myself. I have grown leaps and bounds!"

Many women report that going through a breakup turns out to be an amazing process of self-discovery. "It has become much clearer to me that I have to live life for myself first," says Debbie, age 28. "My breakup made me remember who I really am."

Jenni, age 25, feels the same way. "I never knew who I was because I'd never been alone before. It was the first time since I was twelve that I hadn't had a boyfriend. I learned how to be alone and feel comfortable with myself."

You're Okay After All

Today I travel alone, whenever and wherever I want, and carry each and every one of my bags. Racing solo through the airport and visiting faraway friends has made me feel like a together woman with places to go and people to see. I've turned into someone I've always wanted to be.

You'll have your own moments of epiphany. Something happens, and to your surprise you notice you're feeling better. You might be out to dinner with a few friends when you suddenly realize you're actually having fun. Maybe you're at home just reading a book that you can't put down. It could be a pat on the back from your boss for a job well done. Or it might be a great night out with a new man.

Whatever it is, your life, amazingly, is going on—and going well. As Julie, age 25, puts it, "When Jason and I broke up, I thought it was the worst time of my life. But looking back, our relationship was the worst time of my life. The breakup was the beginning of something good happening."

You've survived hell, and though you weren't always sure you'd make it through the day, you always have. Those tough times have forced you to come to terms with what's really important to you, and what you really want from your life and from your lover. You've made some mistakes, but you've learned from them. You understand others—and yourself—better, and your life is richer and more rewarding as a result. In fact, you've not only survived—you've triumphed!

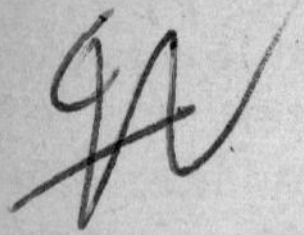

Look for These Books From

COSMOPOLITAN®

THE NICE GIRL'S GUIDE TO SENSATIONAL SEX
by Nancy Kalish
77229-9/$5.99 US/$7.99 Can

WHAT MEN WANT FROM THE WOMEN THEY LOVE
by Ken Carlton
77497-6/$4.99 US/$6.99 Can

ALL THE GOOD MEN ARE <u>NOT</u> TAKEN
by Lisa Simmons
77442-9/$4.99 US/$6.99 Can

IS HE THE RIGHT MAN FOR YOU?
by Sondra Forsyth
77786-X/$5.50 US/$7.50 Can

STAR SPELLS
by Sarah Holcombe
77995-1/$5.50 US/$7.50 Can

WHY DON'T YOU...
by Elizabeth Nix
78671-0/$5.50 US/$7.50 Can

THE DATING GAME
by Ken Carlton
78799-7/$5.99 US/$7.99 Can

Buy these books at your local bookstore or use this coupon for ordering:

Mail to: Avon Books, Dept BP, Box 767, Rte 2, Dresden, TN 38225   G
Please send me the book(s) I have checked above.
❏ My check or money order—no cash or CODs please—for $_____ is enclosed (please add $1.50 per order to cover postage and handling—Canadian residents add 7% GST). U.S. residents make checks payable to Avon Books; Canada residents make checks payable to Hearst Book Group of Canada.
❏ Charge my VISA/MC Acct#_____Exp Date_____
Minimum credit card order is two books or $7.50 (please add postage and handling charge of $1.50 per order—Canadian residents add 7% GST). For faster service, call 1-800-762-0779. Prices and numbers are subject to change without notice. Please allow six to eight weeks for delivery.
Name_____
Address_____
City_____State/Zip_____
Telephone No._____

COS 0897

Parann.
17th 20th Sept.
=

Slever

27th